Globalizing the GATT

Globalizing the GATT

The Soviet Union's Successor States,
Eastern Europe, and the
International Trading System

≡≡≡

LEAH A. HAUS

≡≡≡

The Brookings Institution
Washington, D.C.

Copyright © 1992 by
THE BROOKINGS INSTITUTION
1775 Massachusetts Avenue, N.W., Washington, D.C. 20036

Library of Congress Cataloging-in-Publication Data
Haus, Leah, A., 1960–
  Globalizing the GATT : the Soviet Union's successor states, Eastern Europe, and the international trading system / Leah A. Haus.
    p. cm.
  Includes bibliographical references and index.
  ISBN 0-8157-3504-9 (alk. paper).—ISBN 0-8157-3503-0 (pbk.)
    1. General Agreement of Tariffs and Trade (Organization) 2. Soviet Union—Foreign economic relations. 3. Europe. Eastern—Foreign economic relations. 4. International economic integration. 5. International trade. 6. East-West trade (1945–)
  I. Title. HF1721.H347 1991
  382'.92—dc20   91-45868
                                                                         CIP

9 8 7 6 5 4 3 2 1

The paper used in this publication meets the minimum requirements
of the American National Standard for Information Sciences—
Permanence of Paper for Printed Library Materials, ANSI Z39.48–1984.

₿ THE BROOKINGS INSTITUTION

The Brookings Institution is an independent organization devoted to nonpartisan research, education, and publication in economics, government, foreign policy, and the social sciences generally. Its principal purposes are to aid in the development of sound public policies and to promote public understanding of issues of national importance.

The Institution was founded on December 8, 1927, to merge the activities of the Institute for Government Research, founded in 1916, the Institute of Economics, founded in 1922, and the Robert Brookings Graduate School of Economics and Government, founded in 1924.

The Board of Trustees is responsible for the general administration of the Institution, while the immediate direction of the policies, program, and staff is vested in the President, assisted by an advisory committee of the officers and staff. The by-laws of the Institution state: "It is the function of the Trustees to make possible the conduct of scientific research, and publication, under the most favorable conditions, and to safeguard the independence of the research staff in the pursuit of their studies and in the publication of the results of such studies. It is not a part of their function to determine, control, or influence the conduct of particular investigations or the conclusions reached."

The President bears final responsibility for the decision to publish a manuscript as a Brookings book. In reaching his judgment on the competence, accuracy, and objectivity of each study, the President is advised by the director of the appropriate research program and weighs the views of a panel of expert outside readers who report to him in confidence on the quality of the work. Publication of a work signifies that it is deemed a competent treatment worthy of public consideration but does not imply endorsement of conclusions or recommendations.

The Institution maintains its position of neutrality on issues of public policy in order to safeguard the intellectual freedom of the staff. Hence interpretations or conclusions in Brookings publications should be understood to be solely those of the authors and should not be attributed to the Institution, to its trustees, officers, or other staff members, or to the organizations that support its research.

Foreword

THE DRAMATIC changes in Eastern Europe and the dissolution of the Soviet Union have created new opportunities and challenges, including that of integrating the Eastern countries into the global economy. Such integration will require restructuring Western policies toward economic relations with the East. Though there is general consensus that the West should abandon its previous policy of exclusion and adopt a policy of inclusion, discussions over specifics are likely to generate significant debate within the West in the coming years.

Leah Haus addresses this subject by considering the task of integrating the Soviet Union's successor states and the East European countries into the General Agreement on Tariffs and Trade (GATT), the international trade institution. Through a comparative analysis of the history of negotiations between the Soviet Union, East European countries, and the GATT, she explains current policy problems posed by normalizing relations between these reforming nonmarket countries and the market-oriented trading world. She describes the political and trade policy issues at stake, emphasizing those issues that may generate conflict within the West as discussions move forward.

Leah A. Haus, an assistant professor of politics at New York University, began this study as her Ph.D. dissertation at Brandeis University. She is particularly grateful to Robert Keohane, her thesis adviser, for his comments on various drafts of the dissertation and for his guidance, generosity, and support on a wide range of issues. She also thanks Robert Art and Susan Okin for their help as dissertation advisers. Haus made significant changes to the study after completing the dissertation, and she thanks Ed A. Hewett and John D. Steinbruner for encouraging her to embark on the revisions. She is grateful to John Steinbruner for comments on several versions of the manuscript, to Susan Woodward for comments on the penultimate version, and to Barbara Hinckley for suggestions on various aspects of the manuscript. The author is also grateful to the many current and former officials who agreed to be interviewed for this study. She especially thanks Mr. Linden of the GATT secretariat, who gave his time generously. For collegiality and hospitality, the author thanks Rita Beck, Elizabeth Bussiere, Youssef Cohen, Ben Dickinson, Jennifer and Keith Harding, and Ted Perlmutter.

Jeff Porro and Caroline Lalire edited the manuscript, Vernon Kelley and Michael Levin verified its factual content, Kathryn Breen and Kirsten Soule typed the final version, and Susan L. Woollen prepared the manuscript for typesetting. The index was prepared by Fred Kepler.

The author gratefully acknowledges financial support received from the East European Program of the Woodrow Wilson International Center for Scholars; the Ford Program in European Society and Western Security at Harvard University; the Research Challenge Fund Fellowship, New York University; and the Sachar Travel Fellowship, Brandeis University. Brookings is grateful for support from the Carnegie Corporation of New York, the John D. and Catherine T. MacArthur Foundation, and the Andrew W. Mellon Foundation for its fellowship in Soviet and East European Studies.

The views expressed in this book are those of the author and should not be ascribed to the people acknowledged above, to the sources of funding support, or to the trustees, officers, or staff members of the Brookings Institution.

BRUCE K. MACLAURY
President

January 1992
Washington, D.C.

Contents

Globalizing the GATT

Chapter 1

Introduction

T HE REVOLUTION in Soviet foreign policy in the late 1980s
and the collapse of the Soviet Union in 1991 have had
a profound impact on world politics. The Soviet Union concluded
arms control agreements that eliminated intermediate range nuclear
weapons, cut conventional forces in Europe, and reduced strategic
nuclear forces. Soviet troops withdrew from Afghanistan, and a new
Soviet policy aimed at conflict resolution in developing countries
strengthened the chances for peace in Angola, Cambodia, and the
Middle East. The Soviet government granted formal recognition to
the European Community (EC), an institution that it had once strongly
denounced, and made clear it wanted to be affiliated with such
international economic institutions as the International Monetary Fund
(IMF) and the General Agreement on Tariffs and Trade (GATT). The
Soviet Union did not intervene to prevent the fall of communism in
Eastern Europe or to stop the process of German reunification. The
Warsaw Pact and the Council for Mutual Economic Assistance (CMEA)
collapsed.

The dramatic events of August 1991 demonstrated that Soviet
domestic politics had changed profoundly, too. The hard-liners' attempt to regain control through extraconstitutional means proved to
be a complete failure, reducing rather than increasing the power of
the hard-liners, ending the communist monopoly over political institutions, and opening the path for the dissolution of the Union of
Soviet Socialist Republics in December 1991.

The transitions in the former Soviet Union and Eastern Europe
have ushered in a new pattern of relationships that has been widely
labeled as the post-cold-war world. This emerging new world order
presents opportunities for new forms of international cooperation,

1

as was seen by the approach taken toward the 1990–91 Gulf crisis. But the new realities also pose significant challenges, including the task of integrating the Soviet Union's successor states and Eastern European countries into the global economy. This book examines that challenge by analyzing these Eastern countries' participation in the GATT.

Globalizing the GATT

The GATT is a multilateral trade agreement drawn up in 1947 that has since become the main international institution responsible for guiding the conduct of world trade. The norms and rules of the GATT aim to ensure the maintenance of an open, nondiscriminatory market in which government intervention is minimized and tariffs and prices guide the decisions of private firms.

The General Agreement was drawn up by just twenty-three countries, only twenty-two of which were original signatories.[1] The GATT was thus far removed from the universal trading institution that had been envisioned by the architects of the postwar international economic order, who wanted to create an integrated, nondiscriminatory, global economy. They believed such an economy would foster conditions conducive to prosperity and peace. However, many other countries have since joined the GATT, and there are currently 103 contracting parties. Moreover, twenty-eight other countries maintain a de facto application of the GATT.[2] GATT membership includes several Eastern European countries.[3] Czechoslovakia was an original signatory in 1947 and continued to remain a member, although it adopted a nonmarket economic system shortly after signing. Poland, Rumania, and Hungary joined the GATT as nonmarket economy countries in 1967, 1971, and 1973, respectively. The terms of these countries' accession to the GATT were unusual, however, and differed from the terms of participation for market economy countries.

Despite its large membership, the GATT cannot yet be called a global or universal institution. The countries that have not yet joined include such major powers as Russia, Ukraine, and China. Nonetheless, there are signs that the GATT may move closer to becoming a global trading institution in the future. Accession negotiations are currently under way with several countries, including China and Bulgaria. Mongolia and Albania have informally expressed interest in affiliating with the GATT. The Soviet Union expressed clear interest in increasing its participation in the GATT, and one can expect that its successor states will do likewise.

Purpose of the Study

The main issues concerning the former Soviet Union's and Eastern Europe's relations with the GATT in the post-cold-war world are, first, the task of normalizing the terms of participation for those countries that have already joined the GATT (Poland, Rumania, and Hungary) and, second, the question of membership for those countries that have not yet acceded to the GATT (the Soviet Union's successor states and Bulgaria).

It is often noted that the integration of these countries into the international trading system will depend on economic reform in the East. This book demonstrates that integration will also hinge on Western political objectives and policies.

In past negotiations regarding Eastern participation in the GATT, Western countries have been the key actors, and objective economic developments in the East have in many ways been the least important problems. Instead, political considerations have had the primary impact.

As a result, what will happen in future negotiations regarding, for example, a possible Russian application to join the GATT remains an open question, regardless of what happens to the Eastern economies. While the process of economic restructuring in the East has begun, the task of integrating these countries will also require restructuring Western policies toward trade with the East in accordance with the new political realities of the post-cold-war world.

This study focuses on several key questions. To what extent and in what way do the new political realities require restructuring Western policies toward Eastern participation in the GATT? Will the process of adjustment generate conflicts within the Western alliance? What are the implications of alternative policies that may be taken toward the question of integrating the Soviet Union's successor states into the GATT?

These questions are broached by analyzing the history of Western policies toward Soviet and Eastern European relations with the GATT. This approach helps to give us the background necessary for understanding current policy problems and for adjusting Western policies toward trade with the East in the post-cold-war world. It is impossible to consider the task of restructuring Western policies unless one can fully understand what one is dealing with.

Current issues and policy problems regarding Eastern participation in the GATT have been partly shaped by past events; they did not spring out of nowhere in 1990. It would be too simplistic to presume that the past has no relation to current and future issues, or that no relevant lessons can be drawn from a study of past cases. For example, one cannot understand the marked differences in current issues regarding individual Eastern countries' relations with the GATT without first looking at the historical context and traditional Western perspectives. Furthermore, the Eastern countries did not adopt such autarkic and isolationist policies in the past as is sometimes presumed, but rather attempted many times to participate in international economic organizations like the GATT. The degree of success obtained by individual Eastern governments in their attempts to join the GATT in part depended on Western policies; this will also be true in the future, since the United States and the EC are important participants in the GATT forum. It is therefore imperative to understand traditional Western positions in order to consider the extent to which and the way in which they need to be changed in light of the new realities that are now emerging.

In particular, the book examines negotiations between the key GATT countries and Poland, Rumania, Hungary, Bulgaria, and the former Soviet Union. In mid-1991, none of these countries had "normal" relations with the GATT. Even the countries that are members of the trade institution (Poland, Rumania, and Hungary) have unusual terms of participation that place them in a category often referred to as second-class citizenship. Hence, this book studies all those cases in which the West is faced with the task of formulating new policies in view of the new realities in the East.[4]

The policy question given the most attention here is whether and how to accommodate the participation of the Soviet Union's successor states in the GATT in the post-cold-war world. The negotiations analyzed in this study illustrate some of the issues raised by this question, and share important common features that allow us to draw some general conclusions for dealing with such nonmarket countries as Armenia and Russia. In particular, all the cases examined involve former Warsaw Pact members that applied to develop an affiliation with the GATT when they had nonmarket economic systems.[5]

This case selection does have certain limitations that need to be briefly acknowledged. First, the cases of the sovereign states of the former Soviet Union are more complex than those of the other Eastern countries because some of the states, such as Russia, have a significant role in world politics and have potentially large trading capabilities. Second, the GATT is more frail today than it was at the time that Poland, Rumania, and Hungary acceded. These limitations will be discussed further in the concluding chapter. That chapter shows that a careful analysis of past cases, taking these variations into consideration, can contribute to our understanding of future policies toward the participation of the Soviet Union's successor states in the GATT.

Arguments of the Study

"The Soviet international trading system is at fundamental, practical and philosophical variance with the principles and practices of the GATT." This statement was made by a spokesperson for the Office of the United States Trade Representative in August 1986 when explaining U.S. opposition to the Soviet bid to increase its affiliation with the GATT.[6] The same month a White House spokesperson announced U.S. opposition to the Soviet request because Moscow's "state-supported and controlled economic system" was incompatible with GATT trade rules.[7]

These statements typify public comments made by government officials discussing Soviet bids in the period that is sometimes labeled the new cold war of the 1980s. As John Jackson wrote, "The argument is that the Soviet Union has an economy that is too different from that contemplated by the GATT rules, and that therefore to admit the Soviet Union would do too much damage to the fabric of the GATT system."[8]

Most of the available literature on Soviet and Eastern European relations with the GATT has been written by scholars or officials who specialize in economics. Although some of these authors have taken a far more open-minded approach toward the subject than have government officials in public statements, the focus has nevertheless remained on more technical economic issues.[9]

This book questions that conventional focus on systemic economic differences. It argues that economic policy issues have in the past been less relevant to Soviet and Eastern European participation in the GATT than might be expected from the public record or available literature. Political-security issues have had the predominant impact.

Indeed, political-security considerations have traditionally driven the West's approach toward these trade negotiations. Western policies regarding Soviet and Eastern European relations with the GATT stemmed from the political goals of containing Soviet power and encouraging diversity in the East in order to reduce Soviet influence in that region. I argue that these strategic considerations rather than objective economic conditions in the East have determined whether an individual Eastern country was deemed eligible to participate in the market-oriented international trade institution. Favorable political relations with the West have been a precondition for ensuring that an application for affiliation with the GATT is given serious consideration and is placed on the agenda. Accordingly, as seen in later chapters, the West strongly supported and approved the applications for GATT membership that were submitted by Poland, Rumania, and Hungary in the 1960s and 1970s; the West blocked applications for affiliation with the GATT that were submitted by Bulgaria and the Soviet Union in the 1980s.

The strategic considerations that guided Western policies in the past are now clearly outdated and in need of immediate change. The desirability of moving "beyond containment" has been accepted, and there is no longer a strategic rationale for opposing the Eastern countries' requests for greater affiliation with the GATT. In contrast, political considerations dictate a positive approach toward participation by the former Soviet Union. The integration of the Soviet Union's successor states into the global community is generally viewed as desirable, and one element of this integration involves participation in international economic institutions.

A logical conclusion of the argument that broader political issues are the driving force behind these trade negotiations is that there will be substantial pressure to accommodate the new sovereign states' participation in the GATT in the future, regardless of the pace at which their economies are reformed, and regardless of the opposition that is likely to come from some Western trade policy officials. It will be exceedingly difficult and possibly very unwise to deny the Soviet Union's successor states entry into the main trade institution of the global community if the West wants to encourage the cooperative stance in world politics displayed by the former Soviet Union since the late 1980s.

This book also makes an argument related to the trade policy dilemmas raised by nonmarket countries' participation in the GATT. The economic issues pointed to by government officials and the available literature have usually become significant only after an application is on the agenda and under serious consideration by the GATT. At this stage the negotiations have focused on the terms of participation that are embodied in the agreement (or protocol of accession) reached when a country joins the GATT. The trade policy dilemmas have also been a significant consideration during the subsequent negotiations over the implementation of agreements. In other words, the broader political-security issues that have influenced the criteria for agreement have tended to fade into the background during the negotiations over the terms and implementation of agreements for those nonmarket countries that have been deemed eligible to join the GATT (Poland, Rumania, and Hungary).

The latter phases of the negotiations, which were concerned with trade policy issues, have caused a fair degree of conflict between the United States and Western Europe. The pattern of conflict has been very different from that present in East-West trade negotiations outside the GATT forum. Within the GATT forum, the EC has generally been the main obstructor in the East-West trade negotiations, whereas the United States has generally been the main supporter of the Eastern European countries once it has taken the fundamental political decision to support their applications to join the GATT.

I argue that the transatlantic disputes resulted from pressures and considerations that in many ways had little to do with East-West relations or nonmarket economic systems. Instead, negotiations with the East became enmeshed in broader transatlantic debates over trade policy issues. The particular trade policy dilemmas raised by nonmarket countries' participation in the GATT (for example, how to devise terms of participation that simultaneously upheld two principal norms of the GATT—nondiscrimination and reciprocity) brought broader transatlantic conflicts over nondiscrimination to the forefront of the negotiations.

The United States, with negligible commercial interests at stake, showed little concern for reciprocity and instead championed nondiscrimination. The Western European countries, with somewhat more commercial interests at stake, attached significant importance to reciprocity. They also favored terms of agreement that would allow them to apply bilateral and discriminatory trade practices to Poland, Rumania, and Hungary, thus contradicting the GATT norm of nondiscrimination.

The opposing positions taken by the United States and Western Europe during these particular negotiations in many ways replicated their different positions in numerous other trade negotiations that had nothing to do with East-West trade. Transatlantic disputes over nondiscrimination have a long history dating back to the negotiations over the stillborn International Trade Organization (ITO) in the 1940s, and continuing into the debates over the proliferation of the EC's preferential trade agreements in later years.

The implication of these findings is that the negotiations over normalizing the relations of the Soviet Union's successor states and Eastern Europe with the GATT are very likely to cause conflicts among and within Western governments. The negotiations are likely to become entangled in the broader trade policy debates currently simmering over such issues as nondiscrimination, reciprocity, multilateralism, regionalism, and bilateralism.

In summary, the new political realities of the post-cold-war world will force a fundamental transformation of traditional Western perspectives toward Eastern participation in the GATT. The process of adjustment will be difficult and is likely to generate substantial conflicts within the West.

Overview

Chapter 2 introduces the background material that is essential for understanding the political-security and trade policy issues at stake in negotiations over Eastern participation in the GATT.

Chapters 3 and 4 examine those cases in which Western political-security objectives have led to cooperation between Eastern European countries and the GATT. These chapters explain both the historical origins and the evolution of current policy issues, which center on the renegotiation or normalization of the terms of Poland, Hungary, and Rumania's agreements with the GATT in the post-cold-war world.

Chapters 5 and 6 address those cases in which Western political-security objectives have in the past meant conflict between the GATT and Eastern countries. The broader political issues that have been the driving force behind these negotiations in the past are now clearly outdated. The new political realities dictate cooperation with Bulgaria and the former Soviet Union, indicating that the West will adopt a more open-minded posture toward their applications to participate in the GATT, regardless of the pace at which internal economic reform proceeds.

The final chapter examines the implications of alternative policies that may be adopted toward nonmarket countries' applications to join the GATT in the 1990s. The new independent states of the former Soviet Union–Armenia, Azerbaijan, Belorussia, Estonia, Georgia, Kazakhstan, Kirghizia, Latvia, Lithuania, Moldavia, Russia, Tajikistan, Turkmenistan, Ukraine, and Uzbekistan—are likely to apply to join the GATT in the near future. Formulating an appropriate policy for integrating these countries into the global community is clearly a hazardous task, given the current uncertainty about how events will proceed in some of these countries and for how long and in what form the Commonwealth of Independent States will exist. But failure to consider the implications of possible policy options because of uncertainty would be a fatalistic approach. Indeed, the urgency of the issues stems precisely from the fact that Western policies toward integrating these countries into the GATT (and the global community) might help a little to move the new states' foreign and domestic policies in a desirable direction.

Participation in the GATT by the Soviet Union's successor states is emerging as an important item on the agenda for the 1990s, yet transformation of these countries' economies to a real market system is likely to take some years. Hence, the GATT members will be faced with the challenge of how to integrate (reforming) nonmarket countries into the market-oriented trade institution. Although some trade policy officials who work on GATT issues convey the impression that they would prefer not to even think about this task, the political realities make it an issue that cannot be ignored or wished away. The problem will of course be mitigated if the economic systems of the new sovereign states are speedily, or perhaps miraculously, transformed into a market economy. Until that day arrives, the question of how to integrate nonmarket countries into the international trading system remains significant, and the collapse of the Soviet Union has made that question urgent.

Chapter 2

The Issues at Stake

A FORMER DEPUTY U.S. trade representative for multilateral trade negotiations, when asked if he thought there was a place in the GATT for centrally planned economies such as those of Rumania, China, and the Soviet Union, gave the following response:

No. Certainly not the Soviet Union. Rumania carries out its external trade in some form of market-oriented way. Eighty-five percent of China's trade is with liberal market economies, and it runs its foreign trade sector as a market economy. So one could argue that China has a role in GATT. The question is somewhat moot because China was an original member of GATT before the Communist regime took over. There is no place for the Soviet Union. It's a contradiction in terms. How can you have a centrally planned economy, in which all the decisions are made by the state, in an organization whose fundamental principle is market economy?[1]

Certain aspects of this comment are confusing. In particular, since this statement was made before the Rumanian revolution of December 1989, it is not clear what is meant by "Rumania carries out its external trade in some form of market-oriented way." The statement becomes even more confusing when one learns that the U.S. government gave strong support to the Polish, Rumanian, and Hungarian applications to join the GATT in the 1960s, a time when these countries did not have market economic systems. Furthermore, the American government invited the Soviet Union to participate in other international economic organizations that were envisioned by the architects of the postwar international economic order in the mid-1940s, at a time when the Soviet Union did not have a market economy. Finally, as will be seen in later chapters, the U.S. government invited Soviet participation in the Tokyo Round of multilateral trade negotiations that began in the early 1970s, and approved granting the Soviet Union observer status at the GATT in 1990, even though the Soviet Union had a nonmarket economy.

The question of how to accommodate a nonmarket country to a market-oriented trade institution does indeed pose dilemmas, and part of this chapter is devoted to these trade policy issues. However, it is first necessary to clear up some of the confusion that arises from the public comments of government officials, and to consider the political-security issues that account for the variation in nonmarket countries' relations with the GATT.

The explanation is facilitated by disaggregating the negotiations into several stages to help clarify when different issues predominate in negotiations between Eastern countries and the GATT. The first stage relates to the criteria for agreement and centers on the question whether to accept an Eastern country's bid to develop an affiliation with the GATT. Strategic political issues have dominated during this initial stage and have determined whether an Eastern country's application is placed on the GATT agenda. The second stage, which is concerned with drawing up a protocol of accession for those countries deemed eligible to participate in the GATT, concludes when an agreement is signed and the Eastern country becomes a member of the international trade institution. The third stage centers on the implementation of agreements and focuses on reviewing the extent to which signatories are abiding by the commitments laid out in the protocol of accession. Economic policy issues have surfaced during the second and third stages.

Political-Security Issues

Political issues linked to security have had an important influence over East-West economic relations during the postwar era, and the negotiations regarding Soviet and Eastern European participation in the GATT have been no exception. Indeed, the political-security objectives of the West, rather than systemic economic differences, have been the driving force behind negotiations over Eastern countries' bids to affiliate with the GATT.

Western Policies toward the Soviet Union

Western policies toward the Soviet Union and its allies have, in past decades, aimed to contain or reduce Soviet power through various means, including economics. The use of economics as an instrument of politics has been a feature of both American and Western European policies toward the East since the late 1940s. The United States and Western Europe have supported the continuation of the Coordinating Committee for Multilateral Export Controls (COCOM) since its creation in 1949.[2] Western governments on both sides of the Atlantic have favored imposing an embargo on the export of goods with direct military significance in order to contain the expansion of Soviet power. However, there have been disagreements, too. The United States and West European countries, with different commercial interests at stake and with different notions of the reality of the Soviet threat, have held divergent views about the appropriate degree and nature of linkage between political and economic issues.

The use of economic tools as a means to pursue political objectives in the East has been most strongly practiced by the American government. The basic guidelines underlying the American position toward East-West trade stemmed from the policy of containment, first adopted in the late 1940s after the abandonment of Franklin D. Roosevelt's policy of postwar cooperation with the Soviet Union. Since that time there have been some sharp shifts in the particular strategy of economic containment employed toward the Soviet Union.[3] During the cold war the United States generally opposed trade with the Soviet Union, and the strategy of economic warfare was adopted. An embargo was imposed on the export of goods with indirect military significance, and import regulations were adopted that required the president to withdraw the application of most-favored-nation (MFN) treatment to imports from the USSR and Eastern Europe.[4] This blocked virtually all trade with the Soviet Union.[5] The strategy of economic warfare was replaced by a strategy of inducement in the détente era of the early 1970s, when U.S. policy aimed to give the Soviet Union a stake in the international system. U.S. policy-

makers hoped to change the Soviet conception of international relations and "convince the Russians that it was in their own best
interest to be 'contained.' "[6] However, the administration's attempts
at positive linkage were undermined by the domestic constraints on
U.S. foreign policy. Hopes of increasing trade with the Soviet Union
in return for broader Soviet concessions in the foreign policy arena
were dashed when Congress passed the Jackson-Vanik amendment,
which forbade granting MFN status to a nonmarket country that
restricted or taxed the emigration of citizens.[7] Finally, the new cold
war of the 1980s was characterized by an attempt to revert to the
strategy of economic warfare that had been used at the height of the
cold war in the 1950s.

Western Europe, while supporting the export embargo on goods
with direct military application, has otherwise refrained from employing a strategy of negative linkage or economic warfare toward
the Soviet Union since the mid-1950s. Some of the Western European
governments have at times employed trade as an instrument to pursue political goals in the East, but they have favored positive rather
than negative linkage. For example, in the mid-1960s the French
government, under the leadership of Charles de Gaulle, used economic tools to cultivate a special relationship with the Soviet Union
in order to undermine the rigid, bipolar structure of the cold war
era.[8] Likewise, West Germany adopted a strategy of positive linkage
toward the Soviet Union as part and parcel of its Ostpolitik after
1969. Its aim was to foster economic interdependence to maintain
an atmosphere that was conducive to détente, dialogue, and, ulti-
mately, the resolution of the German question.[9] In contrast, the
British government has tended to strictly separate political-security
issues from economic issues in its relations with the Soviet Union.[10]

The divergent transatlantic approaches toward trade with the Soviet Union have generated some significant conflicts within the Western Alliance, most notably when the Urengoi pipeline dispute ex-
ploded in the early 1980s. The American government failed in its
attempts to persuade, induce, and force Western Europe to adopt a
strategy of economic warfare and forgo the benefits of the pipeline
agreement with the Soviet Union.[11] Western Europe did not share
the Reagan administration's view of the so-called Soviet threat, and
considered that trade with the Soviet Union was a two-way street
from which both West and East could benefit.

Western Policies toward Eastern Europe

To contain the Soviet Union, the West used a range of policies including differentiation, the aim of which was to encourage diversity among the Eastern European countries in order to reduce Soviet influence. In other words, the West's interests in Eastern Europe during the postwar era generally focused on these countries' relations with the Soviet Union. Preferential treatment in the form of economic or diplomatic concessions was granted to those Eastern European countries that pursued foreign or domestic policies that differed from Soviet policies. The use of force was strictly ruled out so as to avoid excessively provoking the Soviet Union in an area that was clearly its vital interest.

The policy of differentiation was most actively employed by the American government, and was first applied to Poland in the late 1950s.[12] The events in Poland in 1956, which culminated in a change in leadership and the introduction of more liberal domestic policies, were regarded as an important development that gave hope for a promising future. The United States accordingly granted Poland credit loans, negotiated sales agreements, and relaxed restrictions on exports of American products to Poland.[13] The United States then extended MFN treatment to Polish goods in December 1960 after concluding that Poland was not "Soviet dominated." This determination made Poland exempt from the provisions of the 1951 Trade Agreements Extension Act, which prohibited granting MFN treatment to imports from countries "controlled by the foreign government or foreign organization controlling the world Communist movement."[14]

Several years later, the United States extended preferential treatment to Rumania to reward it for its relatively independent foreign policy. Controls on the export of U.S. products to Rumania were relaxed in 1964,[15] and Rumania was granted MFN status subject to annual renewal in the context of a bilateral trade agreement reached in 1975. Similar treatment was extended to Hungary in the 1970s to reward the government for its relatively liberal domestic policies, and a U.S.-Hungarian bilateral trade agreement was concluded in 1978.

Some Western European governments, notably France, pursued similar policies. The French government cultivated relations with individual Eastern European countries such as Rumania, Poland, and Hungary in order to overcome the rigid and constraining division of Europe. However, French relations with these countries were consistently subordinated to maintaining good relations with the Soviet Union, and the French government therefore refrained from taking an excessively active approach toward Eastern Europe.[16]

One important exception to the general policy of granting preferential treatment to favored Eastern European countries was West Germany's Ostpolitik after 1969. West Germany, in contrast to other Western governments, adopted a policy that Josef Joffe has labeled synchronization. Good relations with the Soviet Union were viewed as the path to the reunification of Germany. Hence, there was a strong desire to avoid antagonizing the Soviet Union by employing a policy of differentiation. Instead, all Eastern European countries, except for what was then East Germany, tended to be treated equally.[17]

Western Policies toward Eastern Participation in the GATT

The policies of containment and differentiation filtered into the negotiations over Soviet and Eastern European participation in the international trading system. As will be seen in subsequent chapters, the West has supported nonmarket, Eastern European countries' applications to participate in the GATT when strategic political objectives have dictated East-West cooperation. Likewise, the West has blocked applications to GATT when strategic political objectives have dictated conflict. The new political realities of the post-cold-war world dictate cooperation with such states as Russia and Ukraine, and thus these countries' participation in the GATT will be an important item on the agenda in the 1990s.

Trade Policy Issues

The question of how to bring a nonmarket country into the GATT poses some significant trade policy dilemmas, as government officials have noted in public statements. These trade policy issues have usually become important at that stage where an application is placed on the agenda and given serious attention. To fully understand the issues at stake, it is first necessary to briefly introduce the central purpose and norms of the GATT and to then explicate the dilemmas involved in devising terms of participation for nonmarket countries that uphold both the GATT norms of nondiscrimination and reciprocity.

GATT: Trade Liberalization, Nondiscrimination, and Reciprocity

The GATT, along with the International Monetary Fund and the World Bank, is one of the main international institutions designed to guide the conduct of global economic relations. It was established in the 1940s, when the planners of the postwar international economic order set out to create universal organizations that would promote prosperity and peace and prevent a return to the discriminatory practices of the 1930s.

The GATT itself was originally meant to be only a multilateral trade agreement that codified the results of tariff concessions negotiated by twenty-three countries in 1947. GATT signatories agreed to a set of commercial policy principles that were designed to ensure that the tariff concessions were not offset by other trade policy instruments. The GATT was not intended to be an institution, but it took on this role when key Western nations could not agree to set up the planned International Trade Organization. The conflicting interests and positions between and within Western governments had prevented the drafting of a charter for the ITO that would gain sufficient support for ratification. The United States, with a highly competitive economy, had championed nondiscrimination and accordingly favored rules that would outlaw quantitative restrictions and preferential trade agreements. In contrast, Western European governments attached less importance to nondiscrimination and advocated rules that would allow for exceptions to this norm. As Richard Gardner has explained in his classic book on the origins of the postwar international economic order, the numerous conflicts resulted in a proposed ITO Charter that included a complex set of "rules and counter-rules [that] satisfied nobody and alienated nearly everybody."[18] The ITO was stillborn, and the GATT came to fill the vacuum.

The main purpose of the GATT is to encourage trade liberalization. Tariffs are regarded as a legitimate means of import protection, but a GATT central objective has been to reduce tariff rates progressively during multilateral negotiations known as rounds.[19] There has been much success in this regard in past decades, and the average tariff level applied by industrial countries on manufactured goods is now below 5 percent.[20] Nontariff barriers to trade, which involve greater government intervention in the market mechanism than tariffs do, are generally not regarded by the GATT as a legitimate means of import protection. Accordingly, the use of quantitative restrictions and discriminatory quantitative restrictions (the most widespread nontariff barriers that existed when the GATT was drafted) are prohibited under articles 11 and 13 of the General Agreement.[21]

Governments are expected to adhere to the norms of nondiscrimination and reciprocity in their endeavors to remove barriers to trade. Nondiscrimination has often been referred to as the cornerstone of the international trade institution. The drafters of the GATT attached substantial importance to this norm, and the unconditional MFN clause was inserted into the first article of the General Agreement. This obligates contracting parties to apply equal treatment to imports and exports of like products from all other contracting parties. Article 1:1 states:

> With respect to customs duties and charges of any kind imposed on or in connection with importation or exportation or imposed on the international transfer of payments for imports or exports, and with respect to the method of levying such duties and charges, and with respect to all rules and formalities in connection with importation and exportation, . . . any advantage, favour, privilege or immunity granted by any contracting party to any product originating in or destined for any other country shall be accorded immediately and unconditionally to the like product originating in or destined for the territories of all other contracting parties.

The norm of nondiscrimination has been increasingly disregarded by many countries over the years. In particular, regional and bilateral agreements, for example the EC, the European Free Trade Association, and the U.S.-Canadian Free Trade Agreement, have proliferated. Governments have justified these agreements in the GATT forum as practices that fall within article 24 of the General Agreement, a clause that provides for exceptions to the norm of nondiscrimination by allowing the creation of customs unions and free trade areas. As a result of this trend toward regionalism and bilateralism, it may well be argued that "most-favored-nation treatment has, over time, become *less*-favored-nation treatment."[22]

Another source of departure from the unconditional MFN clause has emerged from the increased importance attached to reciprocity. Reciprocity is an important norm of the GATT, despite its mercantilist connotations and its departure from the liberal perspective that underlies the norm of nondiscrimination and many other GATT rules. The severity of this inherent tension between the two principal norms of the GATT—nondiscrimination and reciprocity—depends on the way in which one defines reciprocity. The concept is not defined in the General Agreement, and changes in the meaning and importance assigned to reciprocity have generated an increasing number of practices that depart from the unconditional MFN clause.

In order to understand this issue, it is useful to draw on two terms coined by Robert Keohane: *specific reciprocity* and *diffuse reciprocity*. Specific reciprocity refers to "situations in which specified partners exchange items of equivalent value in a strictly delimited sequence. If any obligations exist, they are clearly specified in terms of rights and duties of particular actors . . . . In situations characterized by diffuse reciprocity, by contrast, the definition of equivalence is less precise, one's partners may be viewed as a group rather than as particular actors, and the sequence of events is less narrowly bounded. Obligations are important. Diffuse reciprocity involves conforming to generally accepted standards of behavior."[23]

Practices that involve specific reciprocity sharply undermine nondiscrimination, whereas practices that reflect diffuse reciprocity are less threatening to nondiscrimination. For example, specific reciprocity is reflected in the conditional MFN clause that was used by the United States until 1923. A tariff concession granted by the United States to country B in the course of bilateral negotiations was only extended to a third country on the condition that the latter grant the United States an equivalent concession in exchange. The concession was withheld from third countries that failed to grant the United States an equivalent quid pro quo. The unconditional MFN clause that was used by many other countries at that time (and later inserted into the General Agreement) reflects diffuse reciprocity. Any concession made by country A to country B in the course of bilateral negotiations is then automatically extended to all other countries that are granted unconditional MFN treatment by country A.[24] Thus, diffuse reciprocity does not involve discriminatory treatment among members of a group providing that each member lives up to its obligations. It may, however, involve discrimination against actors that are not members of the group.

Practices in the GATT forum have traditionally involved a combination of specific and diffuse reciprocity, but in recent years there have been increasing shifts toward specific reciprocity to combat the so-called free rider problem, which occurs when a country reaps the benefits of concessions granted by others without itself reducing obstacles to trade. For example, the unconditional MFN clause was abandoned in the codes on nontariff barriers to trade that were drawn up in the Tokyo Round held in the 1970s. Only signatories to the codes were entitled to the benefits. The beneficial treatment extended to those countries that undertook the obligations of the codes was not automatically extended to those members of the GATT that were not signatories of the codes.

Signs of shifts toward specific reciprocity also include the growing calls for agreements that fall within the category of managed trade, which involves result-oriented (market share) practices rather than opportunity-oriented (market access) practices.[25] Trade flows essentially become planned in advance, and possibly more competitive alternative suppliers from other countries are denied market access. For many years developed countries have applied managed trade when regulating imports in sectors such as textiles. But there have been growing calls for applying managed trade to the sphere of exports.[26] The focus on end results that is associated with managed trade involves precisely defined quid pro quos. This sharply contradicts the norm of nondiscrimination and violates market principles.

New Challenges

Current challenges facing trade policy officials are, in part, a continuation of the long-standing debates pitting nondiscrimination against reciprocity. However, today's challenges are also in many ways different from the concerns of the 1940s, when the General Agreement was drafted. It remains to be seen whether the GATT is flexible enough to change with the times and maintain a role in world trade in the twenty-first century. The deep conflicts prevailing in the current Uruguay Round give cause for skepticism. But it is also appropriate to recall that the GATT system has evolved considerably since the 1940s, and history displays a record of pragmatism and flexibility in the GATT forum.[27]

An example of the evolution in the GATT system can be seen in the shift in the focus of trade liberalization from tariff to nontariff measures. Nontariff barriers to trade, such as government procurement and health and safety standards, became increasingly evident as tariffs and quantitative restrictions were reduced. Much time in GATT negotiations has been devoted to drawing up new codes for coping with these nontariff barriers. Although the General Agreement itself was not amended, codes on nontariff barriers to trade were drawn up during the Tokyo Round of the 1970s and fall within the GATT system.[28] Likewise, trade in services such as banking, transportation, and telecommunications has grown enormously in recent years, but falls outside the scope of the General Agreement, which only covers trade in goods. Attempts are currently being made in the context of the Uruguay Round to draw up regulations that can guide the conduct of trade in services.

Finally, and of central importance to this study, the task of integrating the Soviet Union's successor states into the international trading system presents a significant challenge for the 1990s. Pragmatism and flexibility will have to be applied if the GATT is to have a role in this potentially important area of world trade. This subject was first on the agenda in the mid-1940s, before the onset of the cold war. At that time Western officials adopted a flexible and open-minded approach in their endeavor to create global economic institutions that would help to maintain an integrated world economy, prosperity, and peace. The possibility for fulfilling the universalist goals of the postwar planners is increasingly likely in the post-cold-war world. However, the task of integrating nonmarket countries into the GATT presents trade policy dilemmas that need to be considered.

Nonmarket Countries and the GATT

GATT rules were developed to promote trade between countries with market economies, where relative prices guide the import and export decisions of private firms. In contrast, prices have little influence over decisionmaking and resource allocation in a country with a planned economic system, where the supply of and demand for products are administratively determined. The decisions of enterprises regarding what to produce, how much to produce, in what way, and for whom are determined in advance and specified in a detailed national plan. Prices serve as accounting units rather than as a guide for decisionmaking. Tariffs, which influence prices, likewise have little influence over the quantity, source, and composition of imports. Imports and exports are administratively determined in advance and incorporated into the detailed national plan.[29]

Nonmarket countries thus make it difficult to devise terms of participation that uphold the GATT's conventional norms and rules. The current attempts at economic reform—particularly in Poland, Hungary, and Czechoslovakia—are mitigating these systemic differences. However, despite the recent price reforms, such countries as Russia and Kazakhstan are still far from a market economy, and the process of transformation is likely to take some years.

The problems involved in bringing nonmarket countries into the GATT are clear when one considers the process of accession. The General Agreement does not specify any detailed criteria for accession, and merely states that "a government . . . may accede to this Agreement . . . on terms to be agreed between such government and the contracting parties. Decisions of the contracting parties under this paragraph shall be taken by a two-thirds majority." However, the conventional practice has required that applicants grant tariff concessions as an "entrance fee" to the GATT. The concessions are then extended to all contracting parties equally through adherence to the unconditional MFN clause.[30] This entrance fee thus upholds nondiscrimination and reciprocity. The new member upon accession becomes entitled to MFN status from other contracting parties and thus reaps the benefits of the lower tariff rates and nondiscriminatory treatment associated with MFN status.

This conventional accession procedure is not particularly appropriate for nonmarket countries. Since tariffs have little or no influence over import decisions, other GATT members would not be assured of any increase in export opportunities. Hence, the problem becomes how to devise terms of participation or an entrance fee that does assure contracting parties of increased and nondiscriminatory export opportunities when a nonmarket country joins the GATT. Is it possible to devise an entrance fee for nonmarket countries that simultaneously upholds the norms of reciprocity and nondiscrimination? To put it another way, is it possible to devise a procedure that encourages diffuse reciprocity and thus poses less threat to the norm of nondiscrimination than specific reciprocity does?

There have been some attempts in past decades to devise terms of agreement that encourage nondiscrimination or reciprocity in trade between nonmarket and market countries. These attempts have led to variants of the two methods that were employed in agreements concluded with the Soviet Union in the interwar years. A brief review of these two methods clearly shows the tension between nondiscrimination and reciprocity that arises when formulating trade agreements with nonmarket countries.

The first method, which was the most widely used until the late 1980s, can be labeled the quantitative import commitment. It requires that, in exchange for MFN status, the nonmarket country guarantee it will import a specified amount of products from the market country's firms, regardless of the latter's competitiveness relative to alternative suppliers. This method was first used in the Soviet-Latvian agreement of 1927, where it was agreed that the Soviet Union would purchase 15.4 million rubles worth of Latvian commodities in exchange for receiving MFN status from Latvia.[31] The quantitative import commitment, and variants thereof, is an example of specific reciprocity. It is in many ways very similar to the results-oriented practices associated with managed trade. The quantitative import commitment undermines the market mechanism and threatens nondiscrimination.

The second method can be labeled the commercial considerations clause. It requires that the nonmarket country agree to base its foreign trade on commercial considerations in exchange for MFN status from a market country. This procedure was used in a British-Soviet agreement of 1930,[32] but has otherwise been used very rarely. This method involves little interference with the market mechanism and upholds nondiscrimination. It attempts to ensure that the nonmarket country applies commercial or nondiscriminatory criteria when formulating foreign trade decisions. It thus avoids the pitfalls of the quantitative import commitment. However, it may be difficult to ensure that the nonmarket country abides by its commitment. Moreover, the commercial considerations clause fails to uphold reciprocity. The nonmarket country theoretically upholds nondiscrimination in exchange for the nondiscriminatory treatment associated with MFN status from the market country. But it gives little in return for the greater market access that it receives by way of the lower tariff rates associated with MFN treatment from the market economy country.

In short, it is very difficult to devise terms of agreement with nonmarket countries that simultaneously uphold the norms of non-discrimination and reciprocity. The picture is further complicated for the GATT by the fact that failure to allow nonmarket countries to participate itself undermines the nondiscriminatory, multilateral orientation of the postwar trading system. Exclusion from the GATT leaves the road wide open for countries to apply bilateral and discriminatory trade practices against the East.

As will be seen in following chapters, these trade policy dilemmas have in the past elicited different responses from the United States and Western Europe. When political-security issues have dictated cooperation with an Eastern European country, the United States has adopted an approach similar to that taken in the negotiations over the ITO during the 1940s, championing multilateralism and nondiscrimination. In contrast, Western European governments have emphasized reciprocity and have shown little respect for nondiscrimination in their trade practices toward nonmarket countries.

Conclusion

The move beyond containment in the post-cold-war world indicates that the integration of the Soviet Union's successor states into the GATT will be an important issue on the agenda. The subject raises complex trade policy dilemmas for which there may be no perfect solution. To accommodate the new states' participation in the international trading system, the West may be left with no alternative but to seek a second-best solution and to adopt a flexible, pragmatic, and open-minded approach that permits a departure from one of the main GATT norms. Yet the process of reaching even a second-best solution is likely to generate conflicts within the West. The study of former negotiations between nonmarket countries and the GATT to which I now turn shows that the discussions over trade policy issues have traditionally elicited diverse responses and are likely to become enmeshed in the broader debates over nondiscrimination, reciprocity, multilateralism, regionalism, and bilateralism.

Chapter 3

Poland, Rumania, and Hungary: Accession Negotiations

D E-STALINIZATION in the mid-1950s ushered in a period of increased tolerance for diversity in the East. The changes that followed Stalin's death were nowhere near as dramatic as the events of 1989, and the suppression of the Hungarian revolution in 1956 clearly pointed to the limits of change. Nonetheless, some change did occur, and the previously rigid Soviet grip over Eastern Europe was loosened.[1] The American government's response was to abandon its previous belief in a monolithic communist movement and to instead implement the policy of differentiation, which aimed to encourage further diversity in the East even if that meant cooperating with certain communist governments.

These broader political developments opened the path for Poland, Rumania, and Hungary to develop ties with the GATT in the 1960s. An analysis of the negotiations over these three countries' relations with the GATT reveals certain common themes that provide us with a guide for understanding the key factors involved in normalizing Soviet and Eastern European relations with the GATT in the post-cold-war world.

Poland's Accession to the GATT

Wladyslaw Gomulka's return to power in October 1956 generated high hopes for a new, more liberal era in Poland, and the change in leadership was greeted with enthusiasm in the West. The new political climate set the context for Poland's initial contacts with the GATT in the late 1950s. The government's moves to affiliate with the GATT were part and parcel of its broader effort to expand ties with the West, particularly economic ties.[2]

Polish Concerns

The Polish government's approaches to the GATT were also motivated by a strong desire to increase its export opportunities. Western markets were at that time exceedingly difficult to penetrate. Discriminatory regulations were applied against products from the East, creating what one Polish official referred to as "impenetrable icebergs."[3] Participation in the GATT was seen as a way to overcome this handicap and to obtain wide access to Western markets, because the institution's rules promoted nondiscrimination.[4]

One particular source of concern for Poland was the discriminatory quantitative restrictions (QRs) applied by Western European countries against numerous goods from the East. These import regulations sealed off markets and counteracted the benefits that Eastern European countries obtained from being granted MFN status in tariff matters. The products that were subject to QRs could only be imported from Poland if a quota was opened by the Western European government. Even then the quantity of imports was limited by the amount specified in the quota. Western European governments were under no pressure to remove these discriminatory regulations so long as Poland remained outside the GATT. However, the Polish government hoped that becoming a member of the international trade institution would greatly expand its export opportunities, since GATT regulations prohibited the use of discriminatory QRs.

The second source of concern was the United States. The United States did not apply discriminatory QRs, but instead imposed exceptionally high tariff rates against Polish products. The United States had withdrawn MFN status from Eastern European countries in 1951, making Polish goods subject to the prohibitively high rates of duty established in the 1930 Smoot-Hawley Act.

The Associate Agreement

Poland became an observer at the GATT in October 1957.[5] The Polish government subsequently applied for accession to full membership in March 1959, and then applied to participate in the Dillon Round of multilateral trade negotiations in September 1959.[6]

The applications that were put forward by the Polish government in 1959 received a positive but cautious response from Western governments. The West adopted a supportive approach in order to encourage the political changes that were occurring in Poland.[7] Preferential economic treatment had already been extended through bilateral relations, and Poland's opening to the West likewise provided an opportunity to seriously consider Poland's participation in the multilateral GATT forum. One former official, when discussing the West's position toward Poland's participation in the GATT at that time, explained that "back in 1959 I believed . . . we believed that something really good would happen in Poland."[8] Another former official expressed very similar views and stated that "everyone [was] pro Poland. Much enthusiasm."[9]

The West's support for Poland's attempt to develop further ties with the GATT was nevertheless muted at this stage because of uncertainty about how to deal with the trade policy dilemmas that were raised. In particular, Western officials were unsure how to devise a suitable entrance fee for Poland.[10] Polish officials had made clear that their country had a planned economic system and that there was no likelihood of decentralization in the immediate future.[11] It was therefore evident that reciprocity would not be obtained should Poland merely grant tariff concessions as an entrance fee. There was some uncertainty about how to develop a new procedure. Furthermore, although the broader political atmosphere had improved significantly, it was not yet favorable enough to overcome trade policy concerns.[12]

The West therefore gave an encouraging, but restrained, response in 1959. The Polish government's applications to accede to full membership and to participate in the Dillon Round were not approved. However, the applications were not bluntly rebuffed in the way that the Soviet applications were in the 1980s. Instead, Poland was given some encouragement and an associate agreement, formally called a Declaration on Relations with Poland, was concluded in November 1959.

The associate agreement reached with Poland in many ways reflected the pragmatic and flexible approach that is often applied in the GATT forum. The agreement departed from the conventional GATT practice, which is to allow a nation to graduate directly from observer status to full membership after negotiating a protocol of accession. But the agreement was not unprecedented. Similar agreements had been devised to cope with complicated cases in the past. Associate agreements had also been concluded with Japan in 1953 and with Yugoslavia in May 1959. Moreover, other intermediary stages that fall between observer status and full accession had also been developed for cases that raised very specific problems, that is, provisional accession for Switzerland in 1958.

The accord reached with Poland in November 1959 stated that parties to the declaration, guided by the objectives set out in the preamble to the General Agreement, desired to expand trade on the basis of mutual advantage. It also provided for the possibility of entering into consultations related to the above objective and stated that there would be annual reviews to oversee the implementation of the declaration. Finally, Poland was invited to participate in the sessions of the contracting parties and in the subsidiary bodies established by the contracting parties.[13]

The Kennedy Round

The diverse issues at stake in negotiations over nonmarket countries' relations with the GATT began to become evident when the Polish government applied to participate in the Kennedy Round of multilateral trade negotiations in 1963. This application elicited diverse responses.

The GATT secretariat was attempting to promote the goal of universalism during the 1960s. It was therefore very supportive of Poland's bid.[14] For example, Eric Wyndham White, executive secretary of the GATT at that time, encouraged moves that would broaden the institution's membership.[15] In an address entitled "Looking Outwards," delivered by White in Stockholm in 1960, he discussed the GATT's program for trade expansion that had been launched in 1958 and explained the challenges that this program was designed to address. In one section of the speech he focused on relations between nonmarket countries and the GATT and pointed to the need to seriously consider ways to resolve the trade policy dilemmas raised by these countries' participation in the GATT. He did not say that the trade policy problems posed fundamental barriers to agreement, but emphasized instead the need to consider ideas for resolving the dilemmas. He stated:

> Some of the countries with centrally planned economies are themselves aware of the dangers and limitations of bilateralism and this awareness has translated itself into a renewed interest in

accession to the GATT. Whilst this has been welcomed in principle by the CONTRACTING PARTIES, serious questions have been raised as to whether the GATT rules as they stand could provide the basis for a real balance in trading opportunities and advantages between a contracting party with a centrally planned economy and a contracting party with a free enterprise economy. . . .

It may well be time for resuming the attempt that was made during the I.T.O. trade discussions to spell out trading rules to fit the situation. With full knowledge of my temerity in doing so I will venture to suggest some of the conditions which would appear to be necessary if a country with a centrally planned economy were to offer to a contracting party to GATT—itself a free enterprise economy—conditions of trade comparable to those which the GATT rules are designed to establish. . . .

The enumeration of these possibilities illustrates the complexity and difficulty of the problem. There may be other ways of dealing with it, but it is emerging as a problem which cannot be indefinitely evaded.[16]

White's emphasis on the need to consider ways to resolve, rather than indefinitely evade, the dilemmas was reiterated when he visited Poland the following year. He discussed Poland's relations with the GATT in a speech delivered in Warsaw in June 1961:

This is clearly an area of international economic integration which we cannot neglect and the importance of which we should not minimize. . . . The evolution of relations between Poland and [the] GATT is a matter of great importance and I hope that as these discussions proceed new ideas and imaginative thinking on both sides will contribute to a positive outcome.[17]

White's position on the need to address this area of international economic integration came to be shared by others by the time Poland applied to participate in the Kennedy Round in 1963. In particular, this application, unlike Poland's earlier application to participate in the Dillon Round, received a decidedly positive response from the United States. The American response coincided with the secretariat's position, although the specific considerations leading to the response differed. The favorable U.S. position was influenced by political issues concerning security rather than by a desire to create a universal institution. The strategy of differentiation was becoming more firmly entrenched in U.S. policy toward the East at that time. The Polish government's desire to increase its affiliation with the GATT provided an avenue for advancing that strategy.[18]

Western European governments only partly shared the American enthusiasm. They, too, wanted to give Poland favorable treatment in order to encourage diversity in the East, and they supported Poland's affiliation with the GATT in principle. But Western European governments did not share the American approach toward the trade policy dilemmas. Their concern about how to devise appropriate terms for Polish participation in the multilateral trade negotiations led them to adopt a restrained position that delayed Poland's participation in the Kennedy Round until 1965.[19]

The different transatlantic responses toward the Polish application to participate in the Kennedy Round marked the beginning of what was to become a fairly consistent pattern of alignment in negotiations over trade policy issues—the United States and the socialist country on one side, against the European Community on the other. The supportive U.S. approach contrasted with the cautious Western European position and provided a clear signal that further problems would be encountered in the negotiations over Poland's accession to full membership.

Terms of Accession

The Polish representative to the GATT told a meeting of the council on December 16, 1966, that his government intended to accede to full membership under article 33 of the General Agreement. He asked the chair of the meeting to include this item on the agenda of the next council meeting.[20]

This application received a favorable response from the United States and Western Europe, and it was generally agreed that Poland's accession to the General Agreement should be supported. Thus it was taken as a given that Poland would accede to full membership when the formal negotiations over the terms of accession began in January 1967. This was evident, for example, in an internal U.S. document written at the outset of the formal accession negotiations in January 1967:

It is virtually taken for granted that Polish accession will materialize. Most observers in Geneva believe this will be a Good Thing, in that it is expected to exert liberalizing influences upon the Polish economy, broaden the base of GATT, and stimulate an additional Eastern European country into broader multilateral trade arrangements. . . .

Making due allowances for the rhetoric and artificial courtesy that often attend such formalities in multilateral diplomacy, it is clear from the discussions in the Council and in the corridors that Polish accession to GATT is recognized as being a significant development and is generally supported. . . .

Informed observers in Geneva believe accession procedures themselves might afford some important inducements pulling Poland toward economic decentralization. This would, in turn, presumably tend to orient the Polish economy somewhat more toward the West and somewhat less toward the East, especially in the long run.[21]

The negotiations then turned to the question of the terms of accession, and much attention was given to the problem of how to broach the trade policy dilemmas posed by a nonmarket country's participation in the GATT. The united Western approach disintegrated at this stage. The U.S. government favored drawing up terms of agreement that would preserve nondiscrimination, encourage the development of trade relations with Poland in a multilateral context, and eliminate bilateral and discriminatory trade practices applied to Poland. Western European governments, in contrast, attached much importance to reciprocity and pressed for terms of agreement that would allow them to continue to apply bilateral and discriminatory trade practices to Poland. A former official summarized the views on the two sides as follows: "The U.S. [policymakers] approached these accessions as a multilateral exercise; it was a new experience for them to trade with East European countries, and they saw it in a multilateral framework. The EC saw the accessions as renewed bilateral negotiations."[22]

The discussions concerned with a protocol of accession for Poland focused on several specific issues that were to be the center of attention in later negotiations with Rumania and Hungary. The main stumbling block in all three cases was the discriminatory quantitative restrictions (QRs) that Western European countries applied against products from the East. The other major items under consideration included the nature of the entrance fee that the Eastern European applicant should undertake upon accession, the nature of the safeguard clause that would be inserted into the agreement, and the need to provide for regular reviews to oversee the implementation of the agreement.

The most intense debate during the negotiations was caused by the Western European countries' unwillingness to remove the discriminatory QRs against Polish products. Poland had demanded that these regulations be removed in accordance with the GATT rule of nondiscrimination. But the Western European countries adamantly resisted. Instead, they pressed for terms of agreement that would offer an escape clause from the nondiscrimination rule and thereby allow them to maintain discriminatory QRs. Their position is generally attributed to two factors: their desire to ensure reciprocal gains from trade and their desire to retain national control over economic instruments that served as a tool to pursue security goals in the East.

One group of interviewed officials stressed the first factor, arguing that Western European policymakers considered that it would not be possible to obtain effective reciprocity from Poland in the multilateral GATT framework. The problems of devising an appropriate entrance fee to ensure a quid pro quo led to an unwillingness to grant Poland the benefits of nondiscriminatory treatment associated with GATT membership.[23]

Another group of interviewed officials, including some from the EC, argued that the issue of effective reciprocity did not fully explain the opposition to removing the QRs. These officials argued that there were multiple reasons that have varied over time and among countries. Some in this group referred to the issue of effective reciprocity as a "community ideology" that should not be taken at face value. They indicated that although there were commercial reasons for maintaining the QRs against what have since been termed highly sensitive goods, these concerns were often exaggerated. They also pointed to the fact that many of the QRs were applied against what have since been termed nonsensitive goods, for which the fear of import competition was unfounded. Moreover, the accession agreement was to include a special discriminatory safeguard clause that would provide a mechanism for blocking unwelcome competition. In explaining the Western European position, some officials in this group also generally argued that the QRs served as a means of national control in relations with the East and were used as bargaining chips in bilateral negotiations.[24] This interpretation is supported by the fact that France, in pursuit of the leading role in détente, became, in 1966, the first EC state to remove a large number of its import quotas.[25]

The Western European countries' determination to ensure that the terms of Poland's agreement with the GATT would allow them to maintain their discriminatory QRs generated much antagonism with the United States. It also led to the reemergence of a long-standing transatlantic debate over QRs that had plagued the negotiations over the stillborn ITO in the 1940s. The Americans had traditionally abhorred QRs, with postwar planners in the U.S. Department of State viewing them as the "incarnation of international commercial evil"[26] and the "handmaiden of discrimination."[27] The United States was determined to eliminate bilateralism from trade with Poland. The U.S. position toward discriminatory QRs during the Polish accession negotiations was apparently also influenced by an "anti-EEC" attitude among some U.S. trade policy officials during the 1960s and by the desire "to get things into the GATT framework."[28]

The U.S. government therefore promptly supported the Polish demand that the terms of agreement include a deadline for the removal of the discriminatory QRs in accordance with article 13 of the General Agreement, which prohibits the use of discriminatory import regulations. An internal U.S. document noted the divergent views evident at the early stages of the accession negotiations:

Second session WP [working party] Feb 27 showed fairly clear division of members among three groups, which might be broadly characterized as the liberals, the conservatives, and the non-committal. . . .

In general, liberals want Polish accession to involve minimal derogations from GATT provisions; conservatives desire special provisions and escape clauses so that Polish accession will involve minimal departures from present (bilateral and discriminatory) trade practices. . . . Division between the two groups quite sharp on certain issues.[29]

The transatlantic conflicts escalated as the negotiations regarding the terms of Polish accession proceeded. The establishment of a deadline for the elimination of the discriminatory QRs became the "key U.S. objective."[30] When it appeared that the U.S. determination to establish a deadline was more pronounced than even the Polish resolve to push for it, U.S. officials were instructed to urge the Polish government to take a strong stand and to indicate that the United States was willing to intervene at a high level to overcome obstacles regarding the issue.[31]

U.S. officials focused their attention on attempting to persuade the British government to abandon its opposition to the removal of the discriminatory QRs. The United Kingdom was chosen as the main target because U.S. officials thought the EC's bargaining power would be significantly reduced should Britain, which at that time was not a member of the EC, abandon the united Western European front. The EC would not be able to hold out indefinitely against an American-Polish-British alliance.[32] Britain was also viewed as a potential ally because there were conflicts within the British government that provided possible leeway for influence. According to an American document the policy disputes within Britain centered on the pros and cons of upholding multilateralism in trade with Poland:

> There is real split in British government on bilateral versus multilateral approach to foreign trade. . . . President of Board of Trade had successfully pressed for pressure on Poland with result that in 1966, and 1967 Poland's imports from Britain are exceeding their exports. Lined up against Board of Trade are Bank of England and the Treasury, both of which are inclined towards multilateralism. . . .
>
> Bank of England and Treasury people responded to Board of Trade by pointing out that level of trade is important to Britain and if the common denominator of trade is reduced to bilateralism around the world, then inevitably the level will fall off and Britain will be loser, although in Poland's case they gain at the present time.[33]

The American attempts to persuade the British to adopt a liberal approach failed, despite direct approaches to the government in London. Britain continued to oppose the insertion of a deadline for the removal of the discriminatory QRs in the Polish protocol of accession to the GATT. By June 1967 it was clear that neither the Community nor Britain would abandon the common position it had adopted.[34] Poland conceded to their position that no deadline for the removal of QRs be included in the agreement. The United States was left with little hope of eliminating the QRs once its socialist ally had decided to "take what it can get" from the agreement.[35]

In short, Poland failed to obtain terms of agreement that would have unambiguously entitled it to the benefits of the nondiscriminatory treatment associated with GATT membership.[36] A similar outcome emerged from the discussions over a second item on the agenda—the nature of the safeguard clause that would be inserted into the agreement.

The Polish government was placed under significant pressure to concede to demands that a discriminatory safeguard clause be inserted into the protocol of accession. Such demands were opposed by the United States at the very early stages of the negotiations. However, the U.S. government changed its position by February 1967. U.S. officials apparently decided to support the British demand for a special safeguard mechanism in order to ensure that third countries would not be penalized for actions taken against Polish products.[37] U.S. officials also hoped that the special safeguard clause would make it easier for Western European countries to agree to the insertion of a date for the removal of the discriminatory QRs.[38]

The clause that was agreed upon permitted contracting parties to restrict imports of Polish products if they caused or threatened to cause serious injury to domestic producers of the same or directly competitive products. This clause was a significant departure from the conventional safeguard mechanism embodied in article 19 of the General Agreement. The conventional procedure was nondiscriminatory and permitted a contracting party to restrict imports of given products if they caused or threatened to cause serious injury to domestic producers. The restrictions were to be applied to the specific product regardless of its source of origin, assuring all GATT members of equal treatment and equal market access. In contrast, the clause inserted in the Polish protocol of accession permitted action to be taken against a specific country, Poland. Restrictions could be placed on imports of a Polish product, while imports of the same product from other contracting parties could remain unrestricted.

Another significant issue that emerged during the negotiations over the protocol of accession centered on how to devise a suitable entrance fee for Poland. It was evident that reciprocity would not be obtained should Poland merely grant tariff concessions in accordance with the conventional institutional practice. Instead, there was general agreement that Poland should undertake a variant of the quantitative import commitment that had originated in the bilateral agreements concluded with the Soviet Union in the interwar years. The procedure adopted stated that Poland was to increase its imports from contracting parties by 7 percent each year in exchange for the benefits of GATT membership. This entrance fee reflected a results-oriented, rather than opportunity-oriented, procedure and thus strongly departed from the market-oriented principles of the GATT. In many ways it resembled practices that fall under the category of managed trade.

In summary, Poland's protocol of accession to the GATT specified very different terms of participation from those accorded to market countries. Thus, by the middle of 1991 the GATT was faced with the task of renegotiating Poland's protocol of accession in the post-cold-war world. Not only did the entrance fee and safeguard mechanism differ from conventional procedures, but the ambiguous clause on discriminatory QRs left Poland in a peculiar situation that was to generate many debates in later years. As will be seen in the next chapter, the trade policy conflicts that were present in the accession negotiations continued in the annual reviews that were provided for in the protocol to oversee the implementation of the agreement.

Rumania's Accession to the GATT

Rumania became an observer at the GATT in 1957, at the same time as Poland. However, Rumania adopted a low profile for a long time and did not make significant efforts to develop greater ties with the GATT until the mid-to-late 1960s. It seems that this fairly lengthy delay reflected the lack of encouragement given by the West to Rumania during this period.[39] Rumanian officials themselves were also apparently not eager to rush the matter, and instead wanted to delay further discussions until the completion of Poland's accession negotiations. They viewed Poland as a test case that would provide a precedent to facilitate their own application.[40]

Rumania formally applied to accede to the GATT in 1968, when the Polish accession negotiations concluded.[41] The application received a very favorable response. Rumania then submitted a memorandum on its foreign trade and commercial policy in accordance with conventional institutional procedure. Contracting parties were invited to submit questions on the memorandum, and a working party was set up.[42] The working party held its first meeting in June 1969, after Rumania had provided responses to the seventy-five questions posed on its foreign trade memorandum. Most of this meeting concerned the questions and Rumania's responses on that memorandum.[43]

Rumania received very strong support throughout the subsequent accession negotiations. The era of East-West détente had begun, and the generally favorable political climate filtered into these negotiations in the GATT forum. In fact, the influence of broader political considerations was even more pronounced than in the earlier Polish accession negotiations.[44]

The American position toward the Rumanian accession negotiations was overwhelmingly driven by the policy of differentiation.[45] The Rumanian government was continuing to follow a relatively independent foreign policy, exemplified by Rumania's decision to maintain diplomatic ties with Israel after the Six-Day War in 1967 and to denounce the Warsaw Pact invasion of Czechoslovakia in 1968. American relations with Rumania were improving rapidly, and Bucharest was the first Eastern European capital visited by Richard Nixon when he became president. Indeed, Nixon's visit to Bucharest in August 1969 marked the first-ever state visit by an American president to a communist country.[46]

The negotiations between Rumania and the GATT were no exception to this general trend. One former American official, when discussing the negotiations in the GATT forum, explained that "the Rumanian agreement was a farce. It was a totally political agreement to encourage an independent foreign policy from the Soviet Union."[47]

Western European governments likewise adopted a favorable approach toward the Rumanian application in light of their desire to encourage the government's independent foreign policy.[48] However, as in the Polish accession negotiations, Western Europe adopted a more restrained approach toward the trade policy matters raised by Rumania's accession to the GATT.

The discussions over trade policy issues focused on items similar to those raised in the Polish accession negotiations. Once again the major conflict centered on the discriminatory QRs that Western European countries applied against products from the East. Rumanian officials initially demanded that the discriminatory QRs be removed in accordance with article 13 of the General Agreement.[49] The EC member states were firmly opposed, and at first it seemed they wanted the Rumanian agreement to include the same clause that had been inserted in the Polish agreement. The Western European countries apparently feared that if they granted Rumania more lenient terms they would create an undesirable precedent. Leniency would pressure them to concede to even more generous terms in possible future negotiations with such other countries as Hungary and Bulgaria.[50]

The conflict between Rumania and the EC showed few signs of resolution throughout 1969. The same pattern of alignment that occurred in the Polish case began to emerge. The American representative apparently gave Rumania substantial support, and was at times so vocal that he deflected the EC's antagonism away from the EC and Rumania. Instead, it seemed that the fight over QRs was at times largely between the United States and the EC, with Rumania left as a quiet bystander. Western European representatives "were mad" at American officials for their active role in pursuing the interests of a communist country. American officials were told "to either shut up, or not to look like the East European countries' best friend."[51]

The EC's hostility toward the American stance was heightened by the fact that the United States itself would not be legally bound by any agreement between Rumania and the GATT. American domestic legislation prohibited the United States from complying with a multilateral agreement extending MFN treatment to Rumania in accordance with article 1 of the General Agreement because section 231 of the 1962 Trade Agreements Expansion Act prevented granting MFN status to products "of any country or area dominated or controlled by communism." The United States therefore made it clear that it would have to invoke article 35 of the GATT, which permits the nonapplication of the General Agreement between two contracting parties if "either of the contracting parties, at the time either becomes a contracting party, does not consent to such application." Hence, none of the rights and obligations of the multilateral agreement would apply to relations between the United States and Rumania.[52] This specific source of tension between the United States and the EC was to reemerge in the Hungarian case. It had not been relevant in the Polish case because Poland had been exempted from the terms of the 1962 Trade Agreements Expansion Act and was granted MFN status by the United States.[53]

Rumanian officials began to show some signs of flexibility toward the problem of QRs by November 1969. They insisted that the agreement include a date to specify a deadline for removal of the discriminatory QRs, but let it be known that this date could be relatively far in the future. Ironically, the Rumanian position was at this stage somewhat more flexible than the position adopted by some other countries, including the United States, Canada, and Australia. All three wanted to see the discriminatory QRs removed with the least delay and favored setting up a precise timetable for the elimination of the discriminatory regulations. The Community maintained an unyielding stance, and the EC member states continued to insist that the "Polish formula" be reused. They refused to consider the insertion of a deadline for the elimination of the QRs.[54]

This stalemate began to break at the end of 1969. Progress ensued, facilitated by informally linking the negotiations between different parts of the overall agreement. Rumanian officials agreed to some of the EC's demands on the issue of QRs in exchange for Community support for the Rumanian position that its entrance fee to the GATT be less specific than the very burdensome Polish commitment.[55] This reciprocal exchange of benefits during the negotiation contributed to an agreement that was almost devoid of reciprocity because few rights and obligations were exchanged. The Community undertook few precise commitments to remove the discriminatory QRs, and Rumania undertook a relatively lenient commitment as an entrance fee to the GATT.

Progress toward agreement between the Community and Rumania was, however, temporarily set back by substantial disagreement within the EC. The differing positions became clear at an internal Community meeting held in December 1969, where a dispute emerged between France and the Netherlands. The French delegate favored an ambiguous compromise clause on QRs for the Rumanian protocol of accession. The clause would have been partly a concession because it would have set a specific deadline for the removal of discriminatory

QRs. However, the clause would have also included exceptions to the general rule that the QRs be removed by the specified date.[56] This compromise proposal was opposed by the Benelux countries, who argued that the clause imposed an imbalance in obligations between the individual EC member states during the implementation phase.[57]

It is possible that these different positions resulted from a variation in the importance that the individual EC member states attached to the broader political-security implications of concluding a successful agreement with Rumania. France may have been more amenable because political considerations had a relatively large impact on the French position toward trade with the East at that time. However, internal Community squabbles over QRs were to recur in many future negotiations with other Eastern European countries. It is therefore appropriate to briefly discuss another possible cause for the intra-Community quarrels.

The EC as a whole did not apply discriminatory QRs to Eastern Europe. Individual member states did, and the amount each applied varied. Thus the individual members had different interests in the outcome of negotiations with the East on discriminatory QRs. Those with the most discriminatory QRs tended to be the most reluctant to give them up. The issue was further complicated by general, or nonspecific, quotas. These technically did not discriminate against Eastern Europe because EC states applied them both to Eastern European countries and to at least one other market-economy GATT member, most commonly Japan. But they clearly did affect East-West trade, and individual EC members also applied varying amounts of such quotas. While France, for example, did not apply many discriminatory QRs, it did use a lot of general quotas. Since general quotas would not be considered discriminatory QRs, they would not be subject to examination during the implementation phase of an accession agreement. Thus a QR applied by France against products from the East and just one other GATT member would remain beyond the scope of any agreement reached with an Eastern European country. Clearly France's interests were much different from those of states that used a lot of discriminatory QRs and not many general quotas.

These latter countries (for example, Britain in later bilateral negotiations between the EC and Hungary in the 1980s) believed they were being penalized for maintaining a liberal policy and employing few quotas against market-economy GATT members.[58] This was the argument put forward by the Benelux countries during the internal Community meetings held to discuss the Rumanian protocol of accession to the GATT. They stressed that countries with relatively few general quotas applied against market-economy GATT members would bear a disproportionate share of the burden during the implementation phase of the agreement with Rumania.[59]

The dispute between the member states persisted over the next year and a half. It became clear by April 1970 that the Rumanian government would agree to the compromise clause supported by the French government and would concede to the demand that the clause include provisions for exceptions. However, the Benelux countries continued to oppose the suggested clause. By the early summer of 1971, the clause on discriminatory QRs was the only remaining stumbling block to Rumania's accession to the GATT. All other aspects of Rumania's protocol of accession had been settled. Substantial progress was made at a working party meeting held in the GATT forum on June 14 to discuss the subject. The compromise proposal was deemed acceptable by Rumania and other major contracting parties, including the United States and Canada. The compromise clause also had the strong support of three EC member states at this time—France, Germany, and Italy.[60]

The Benelux countries, however, continued to oppose the compromise clause when it was discussed at an internal Community meeting held on July 1. During this meeting the French, Italian, and German representatives urged the Benelux delegation to accept the clause. They stressed that Rumania would have a strong case for blaming the Community for the stalled negotiations in the GATT forum if the Community rejected the proposed clause. The undesirable broader political implications of this scenario were also noted.[61] The Benelux countries were left isolated. The Benelux governments reconsidered the matter, and two weeks later they approved the compromise clause.[62]

The secondary issue during the Rumanian accession negotiations centered on how to ensure reciprocity from the nonmarket country in exchange for MFN status. The Rumanian government was willing to undertake a variant of the quantitative import commitment as an entrance fee to the GATT. But it firmly opposed the very specific procedure that had been devised in the Polish case and clearly indicated that Rumania would not agree to increase imports by a fixed percentage annually.

The Rumanian representative initially made several references to the need to link exports and imports. He also proposed that the entrance fee should require Rumania to spend the hard currency earned from exports to contracting parties on imports from contracting parties.[63] This proposal received a generally negative response. Other delegates believed that Rumania would undertake no obligations as an entrance fee should this proposal be accepted, because Rumania was likely to spend any available hard currency on imports from the West regardless of whether it was a member of the GATT.[64]

The major contracting parties, although skeptical of the Rumanian proposal, were divided about how to resolve the dilemma. At the early stages of the negotiations the United States, Canada, and Japan wanted to reuse the procedure devised for Poland.[65] In contrast, the EC supported the Rumanian demand that the commitment be more general than the very specific and burdensome Polish commitment. The Community wanted to ensure that the commitment departed from the conventional procedure used for market-economy applicants because this would clearly present Rumania as a country with a different economic system. It would therefore also provide the Community with some basis for justifying the maintenance of discriminatory QRs.[66] However, the Community was otherwise willing to adopt an open-minded approach and showed relatively little concern about the precise nature of the commitment. As explained above, the Community's support for the Rumanian demands on the entrance fee was given in exchange for Rumanian flexibility on the clause related to discriminatory QRs.

The dispute over Rumania's entrance fee to the GATT was resolved in the spring of 1971. The new rule agreed upon was in line with the Rumanian desire to avoid the specific commitment undertaken by Poland. It merely stated that Rumania "firmly intends to increase its imports from the contracting parties as a whole at a rate not smaller than the growth of total Rumanian imports provided for in its Five-Year Plans."[67] Finally, the Rumanian protocol of accession, like the Polish accord, included a discriminatory safeguard clause and provided for biennial reviews to oversee the implementation of the agreement.

Hungary's Accession to the GATT

Hungary initially applied for observer status shortly after Poland and Rumania, in 1958. However, the suppression of the Hungarian revolution in 1956 had created an unfavorable political climate, and there was little chance of Hungary's bid succeeding. The application was withdrawn.[68]

Political relations between Hungary and the West changed substantially during the next decade. The Hungarian government, under the leadership of Janos Kadar, had embarked on its own variant of pragmatic communism in the early 1960s, symbolized by Kadar's famous pronouncement that "whoever is not against us is with us." The pragmatic approach accepted the leading role of the Communist party as a fact of life that was not to be called into question. The 1956 revolution was not to be repeated. However, Kadar encouraged political relaxation and economic reform in order to improve the population's life style under communism.[69] The movement toward economic reform culminated in 1968 with the introduction of the new economic mechanism (NEM), which introduced an economic system that has been characterized as one of "neither plans nor markets."[70] It was designed to shift many responsibilities from central authorities to individual enterprises. The price system was reformed to allow prices to play some role in the newly decentralized decisionmaking processes. The market, however, was to remain highly regulated.

The new political climate in the late 1960s provided an opportunity for Hungary to renew its approaches to the GATT. This time it received substantial encouragement. Hungary's application for observer status at the GATT was approved in December 1966.[71] Political considerations had an underlying influence throughout the subsequent accession negotiations, and the desirability of Hungary's affiliation with the GATT remained unquestioned during the negotiations over terms of participation. Western governments viewed the domestic liberalization occurring in Hungary as a development to be encouraged in accordance with the strategy of differentiation. Moreover, the broader détente in East-West relations at the end of the 1960s provided a particularly favorable atmosphere.[72]

The NEM, Tariffs, and the Entrance Fee

The negotiations over the terms of Hungary's participation in the GATT shared some important features with the Polish and Rumanian cases and elicited fairly predictable responses from the West. Once again, the United States championed nondiscrimination and gave significant support to the socialist country in its fight with the EC. However, some of the specific items under discussion in the Hungarian accession negotiations differed from the previous cases because of the introduction of the new economic mechanism in 1968. According to the Hungarian representative, the NEM made it appropriate for Hungary to engage in tariff negotiations as a suitable entrance fee to the GATT.

Hungary presented itself to the GATT as a country with a unique economic system, which it described as a "socialist planned economic system." According to the Hungarians, "the plan conceptions [were] realized by economic regulators and not by obligatory plan directives," and the new customs tariff was to play a role in trade policy.[73] The Hungarian representative made it clear from the outset that his government expected these particular circumstances would be taken into account during negotiations and that Hungary would be viewed as a specific individual case. This position was articulated by the Hungarian representative at a session of the contracting parties in 1967, when he stated, "As to the form of a possible collaboration, we are not bound by any pattern and we think that the case of each country should be considered on its own merits. Therefore, we do not think that solutions found in one case should apply automatically to any other."[74]

The subject of Hungary's accession to the GATT was discussed at more length in the spring and summer of 1968 in informal meetings between representatives from Hungary, the major contracting parties, and the secretariat. During this period the Hungarian representative reiterated his hope that his country would not be lumped together with other socialist Eastern European countries. He also explained that Hungary's plan was only indicative and that government intervention was insufficient to allow Hungary to undertake any commitment requiring a fixed, guaranteed increase in imports. In view of these particular circumstances, he proposed that Hungary should participate in tariff negotiations as an entrance fee to the GATT—an argument that was to reemerge in the discussions regarding Bulgaria's bid to join the GATT in the mid-1980s.

The Hungarian demand that tariff concessions be accepted as a legitimate entrance fee received a reserved and noncommittal response in these initial informal discussions. Hungary's case raised trade policy issues that had not been encountered before. Key GATT countries were uncertain how to respond to these new dilemmas, given the lack of knowledge about the role of the tariff and import licensing system in the Hungarian economy under the NEM. Hungary was advised to apply officially for accession so that a working party could be established to examine these trade policy issues.[75]

The Hungarian government accordingly applied to accede to the GATT, and the issue was discussed at a meeting of the council in July 1969. Many delegations welcomed and supported the application, and indicated that Hungary's decision to join the GATT would contribute to further multilateralism in trade. A working party was established with the standard terms of reference—to examine the application and to submit to the council recommendations that might include a draft protocol of accession. Hungary was asked to submit a memorandum on its foreign trade system in accordance with conventional institutional practice. In addition, the secretariat was asked to write a paper on the operation of the Hungarian tariff and its role in the Hungarian economy.[76]

The working party first convened in December 1970. In the intervening period the Hungarian foreign trade memorandum had been circulated, contracting parties had submitted questions on the memorandum, and written answers had been distributed in response to the questions. Finally, the secretariat's paper on the Hungarian tariff was also circulated to members of the working party. The secretariat's study refrained from passing any judgment on the effectiveness of the Hungarian tariff, because that task fell outside its competence. The paper nevertheless said in the conclusion: "At present, it can fairly be said, however, that the functions of the tariff and the rate of customs duty are somewhat different than those in the majority of the developed GATT countries."[77]

At the time of the first working party meeting quite a few contracting parties expressed doubt about the Hungarian proposal that tariff concessions be accepted as a legitimate entrance fee. No contracting party vocally supported the Hungarian proposal at this early stage of the negotiations. The Hungarian representative, however, showed absolutely no signs of flexibility. From the start he "flatly refused" to consider proposals that Hungary should undertake some form of quantitative commitment.[78]

As the negotiations progressed, the trade policy issues raised by the Hungarian proposal generated the same pattern of alignment as that seen in the negotiations over discriminatory QRs. The EC states opposed the Hungarian request that tariff concessions be accepted as a legitimate entrance fee, whereas the U.S. government strongly supported the Hungarian proposal.

The opposition from the EC states stemmed from a desire to uphold reciprocity and to devise an entrance fee that would ensure increased export opportunities. The EC states were skeptical about the role of the Hungarian tariff and did not believe that any meaningful quid pro quo would be obtained should Hungary merely grant tariff concessions. They therefore put forward numerous proposals for Hungary to undertake some form of a quantitative commitment instead of, or in addition to, granting tariff concessions.

The Hungarian proposal elicited a much more positive response from the United States for several reasons. First, the commercial considerations that guided Western European approaches were less relevant for the United States. Although neither Western Europe nor the United States had substantial trade with Hungary, commercial interest was nevertheless greater for Western Europe. In 1970 trade with Hungary accounted for 0.041 percent of total U.S. trade and 0.328 percent of total EC trade.[79] With little at stake, the United States showed little attachment to the norm of reciprocity.

Second, although the policy of differentiation led Western Europe to support Hungary's accession in principle, the broader political issues had far more influence over the American position. The United States wanted to reach terms of agreement that would maximize the possibilities for encouraging further reform within Hungary. American officials were also persuaded by a related argument stressed by the Hungarians during informal discussions. Hungarian officials had repeatedly argued that if the terms of agreement gave some recognition to the NEM, the bargaining power of reform-oriented policymakers in domestic policy conflicts would increase.[80] Hungary would be obliged to adhere to the market-oriented rules of the General Agreement should the protocol of accession categorize Hungary as a market country. Reform-oriented policymakers could point to the international commitment in domestic disputes. This argument won over American officials, who therefore favored accepting the proposal that tariff concessions be considered a legitimate entrance fee.[81]

Finally, American officials were less skeptical than others about the effectiveness of the Hungarian tariff, apparently believing that the tariff played some role in the Hungarian foreign trade system.[82] These considerations were noted in an internal American document as follows:

> Hungarian tariff schedule would appear [to] play [a] growing role in regulating imports. Moreover, it is [a] key feature of [the] country's economic reforms, which are characterized by movement toward economic independence, experimentation, and adoption [of] market features. Accession to GATT under appropriate terms could further such tendencies, which it [is] in our interest to encourage.[83]

The Hungarian demand that tariff concessions be accepted as an entrance fee was met, despite initial skepticism in many quarters and despite significant and persistent opposition from the EC states. This outcome resulted from a combination of favorable conditions. In particular, the final approval of the application hinged on the support given by the United States. The American representative gave the socialist country substantial backing—a sight that was by now fairly common in negotiations over terms of Eastern European countries' participation in the GATT. U.S. officials apparently enlisted the support of other contracting parties, including Canada, Switzerland, and Australia, to isolate the Community and overwhelm the opposition.

The approval of Hungarian tariff concessions was also facilitated by a certain degree of support received from the Commission of the European Communities. As in the Rumanian accession negotiations, implicit reciprocity between the Commission and the socialist applicant was applied during the negotiations over the terms of Hungary's participation in the GATT. The Commission representative adopted a more flexible stance toward the issue of the Hungarian entrance fee in order to dampen Hungarian demands in the sphere of discriminatory QRs. The general tactic adopted by the Commission was to place little pressure on the Hungarians on all issues except the two subjects that were of most concern to the Community—the clause on discriminatory QRs and a discriminatory safeguard clause.[84] This strategy was evident at a working party meeting in June 1971, when the Community representative said that the EC was willing to accept Hungarian tariff offers, but that this agreement was conditional on the elaboration of an acceptable agreement on other issues, primarily QRs and safeguards. He made it clear that the Community would not enter into tariff negotiations with Hungary until a satisfactory protocol of accession was drawn up.[85]

Finally, agreement to Hungary's demand that tariff concessions be accepted as a legitimate entrance fee was also attributable to the negotiating skills of the Hungarian representative. As one official explained, the Hungarian representative was a "very powerful character, and it's undoubted that his character had an influence on the negotiations." Another official described the Hungarian negotiator as "playing games very well. He could confuse everyone."[86] The Hungarian representative's stance was to give a completely inflexible response to all the proposals that Hungary should undertake a quantitative import commitment. Every time such a proposal was put forward, he replied with a short, explicit, and firm "No."[87] When asked why the Hungarian demand was approved despite significant opposition, one official from an EC member state explained, "We had no choice; he refused everything."[88]

Back to the East

The second key demand made by the Hungarian representative was that the protocol of accession include an escape clause that would allow his country to continue the traditional regulations that it applied in trade relations with other Eastern European countries. This issue had been less relevant in the Polish and Rumanian cases because Poland and Rumania had presented themselves as countries with planned economic systems, and they conducted trade with both West and East through the central economic plan. In contrast, Hungary presented itself to the GATT as a country where the tariff played a role in determining imports from the West, while it continued to conduct its trade relations with the socialist countries through a central economic plan. Some contracting parties questioned why Hungary did not apply its tariff to products from socialist countries and expressed concern that Hungary's failure to do so might result in discrimination against products from market-economy members of the GATT.

The Hungarian representative clearly stated that affiliation with the GATT was not to interfere with Hungary's political-economic relations with the East and that Hungary had absolutely no intention of changing existing regulations. He explained the Hungarian position as follows:

> As to why Hungary has a vital interest to have good trade relations with Comecon [CMEA] countries, I invoke two reasons: an historical one and a geographical one.
>
> Geographically, the Comecon countries happen to be our neighbours. . . . I do not think that the share of our neighbouring countries is excessively high. In our Memorandum, we pointed out that historically the countries which are now members of the Comecon represent the same share of our imports, except the Soviet Union with which the former Hungarian regime had abolished all trade. Now, the Soviet Union's share in our import is about 40 per cent exactly the percentage which some of her neighbours have with the Federal Republic of Germany.
>
> Then the historical facts are well-known to all. I do not think it will serve a useful purpose to dwell on what these historical reasons are. I might only hint that the historical reasons lie not only and not exclusively in the eastern part of Europe.[89]

The matter was resolved by including an escape clause in the agreement that permitted Hungary to continue existing trade practices with planned-economy countries, subject to a Hungarian commitment that it would not use these practices to discriminate against products from other contracting parties.[90]

The Hungarian representative was less successful in obtaining the desired terms of agreement with regard to the issue of discriminatory QRs applied by Western Europe against products from the East. The subject generated the usual cooperation between the United States and the socialist applicant, and the usual conflict with the Community. The dispute over QRs was once again the last issue to be resolved in the negotiations.[91]

The Hungarian representative initially asked for immediate removal of the QRs. He did, however, express a willingness to accept a transition period on the condition that any QRs remaining after this time be subject to a request for a waiver under article 25 of the General Agreement, which permits the contracting parties to waive an obligation imposed upon a contracting party in exceptional circumstances. The main Hungarian concern was that the QRs not be legalized and that countries maintaining discriminatory QRs be required to appeal for a waiver. It appears that the QRs were more important to the Hungarians as a symbol of discrimination than as a significant obstacle to trade.[92]

The Hungarian request predictably met with opposition from the EC. The EC made it clear that it would show no more flexibility than in previous cases. The Community insisted that the agreement include provisions for exceptions to a general rule that QRs be removed by a specified date, and proposed that the Rumanian formula be reused.[93] The dispute over QRs remained the major stumbling block to agreement by November 1971. The Hungarian government had little choice but to accede to the broad thrust of the Community's proposal.[94]

There was general recognition by this stage that the clause on QRs would largely accede to the Community's position. However, both Hungary and the United States continued to fight with the Community about the specific words of the clause. The American representative was instructed to persist in his effort to ensure that the clause put more pressure on the EC than it desired. The United States insisted on the inclusion of a phrase that would require countries to at least prove "exceptional circumstances" to justify any QRs remaining after the transition period. Agreement was reached when the Community concurred that the second paragraph of the clause would begin with the phrase "for exceptional reasons."[95]

The Community (in this instance supported by the United States) also insisted that the protocol of accession include a discriminatory safeguard clause.[96] The demand was accepted by the Hungarian representative after much protest. However, he stressed that this acceptance was in anticipation of the early elimination of the discriminatory QRs.[97] Finally, as in the cases of Poland and Rumania, the protocol of accession included a provision for biennial meetings to oversee the implementation of the agreement.

The Hungarian protocol of accession, in short, included a curious mixture of clauses that reflected Hungary's delicate balancing act between East and West, and between plans and markets. The protocol of accession placed Hungary in a somewhat unusual category. The safeguard mechanism was similar to the clause inserted in the agreements with other nonmarket, Eastern European countries. The clause on QRs was ambiguously phrased. The entrance fee was the same as that paid by all other market-oriented Western countries. To confuse matters further, Hungary was permitted to continue to conduct trade relations with the East through conventional planning mechanisms. This strange mixture of ingredients was to cause substantial disputes in subsequent years.

Summary

The increased tolerance for diversity in the East under Stalin's successors provided an opening for the West to pursue the policy of differentiation, whose ultimate goal was to reduce Soviet power in the region. These broader strategic considerations dictated a cooperative position toward Poland, Rumania, and Hungary, and the West was united in its desire to bring these nonmarket countries into the GATT. Political issues deemed these specific countries eligible to participate in the GATT and placed their participation on the GATT agenda. The desirability of including these countries in the GATT remained unquestioned throughout the accession negotiations in all three cases.

The trade policy issues discussed during the accession negotiations elicited diverse responses on the two sides of the Atlantic and led to the reemergence of long-standing transatlantic disputes over multilateralism and bilateralism. In all three cases the United States upheld nondiscrimination and pressed for terms of agreement that would eliminate bilateralism and bring economic relations into the GATT framework. In contrast, the Community favored terms of agreement that would permit members to apply bilateral and discriminatory practices against the Eastern European members of the GATT.

The trade policy dilemmas resulted in terms of participation that were unusual and placed these countries into a category of second-class citizenship. Although the three protocols of accession had specific differences (most notably with regard to the entrance fee), all three agreements failed to guarantee that the Eastern European countries would gain the nondiscriminatory treatment associated with GATT membership. The arrangements all included a discriminatory safeguard mechanism. Of more importance, all the agreements failed to resolve the dispute over the discriminatory QRs applied by Western Europe against products from the East. The Polish agreement was particularly weak in this regard because it did not even include a deadline for removal of the QRs. But the Rumanian and Hungarian agreements also left the matter ambiguous. The trade policy disputes were not really resolved during the accession negotiations, but were placed aside because of the strong desire to reach agreements that would bring these countries closer to the West. Many of the disputes resurfaced in subsequent years, as is seen in the following chapter.

Chapter 4

Poland, Rumania, and Hungary: The Implementation Stage

POLAND'S, Rumania's, and Hungary's accessions to the GATT were important symbolic steps toward breaking down barriers that separated these countries from the global community. The GATT provided a forum for increasing communication with other governments and for exposing Eastern officials to the market-oriented principles that underlie the international trading system. But membership in the GATT gave few tangible benefits, and some of the trade policy disputes that had plagued the accession negotiations became the source of much conflict during the subsequent implementation stage.

The protocols of accession included provisions for periodic meetings to review the extent to which the signatories were complying with the obligations laid out in the agreements and to oversee the development of trade.[1] These meetings were quickly transformed into heated debates that became enmeshed in broader conflicts over multilateralism and bilateralism. Once again the trade policy issues involved generated significant dispute between the United States and the European Community.

Discriminatory Quantitative Restrictions

Not surprisingly, the major dispute during the periodic reviews centered on the discriminatory QRs that certain contracting parties applied against products from the East. The conflicts over this issue had not been resolved during the accession negotiations, and the relevant clauses inserted into the protocols of accession were ambiguously phrased. Governments that applied QRs had been pressured to undertake firmer commitments in the Hungarian and Rumanian accords than in the Polish accord. The Hungarian and Rumanian accords included a deadline that was to serve as a target date for removal of the restrictions. The Polish accord, on the other hand, merely stated that the question of establishing a deadline would be discussed during the course of the third annual consultation and at all subsequent consultations until a date was agreed upon.[2] However, the precise words of the clauses in all three protocols left room for alternative interpretations about the extent to which and the speed at which the QRs were to be removed during the implementation stage.

Problems of Ambiguity

These problems of ambiguity were intensified by the very scanty information initially supplied by some of the countries that applied the restrictions. Lack of information ruled out evaluating the extent to which the restrictions were indeed being removed. The European Community provided particularly fuzzy information in the earlier years, and many delegations considered that the EC data was inadequate for the task at hand. For example, in 1971 the European Community reported very broad figures that included all restrictions (discriminatory and residual) that affected imports from Poland. According to these data, 16 percent of the EC's imports from Poland ($55.6 million) were covered by discriminatory and residual restrictions in 1971.[3] Because all restrictions (discriminatory and residual) were listed as a single item, it was impossible to ascertain whether any progress had been made toward liberalizing discriminatory QRs.[4]

The following year the Community changed the manner in which the data were presented in order to accommodate some of the criticisms it received. The statistics on the notifications were limited to discriminatory restrictions. According to the data supplied by the EC, $42.2 million of imports from Poland were covered by discriminatory restrictions in 1972. However, the Community failed to supply similar information for 1967, thus making it impossible to assess the progress that had been made since Poland's accession to the GATT.[5] The Community also failed to provide data for the individual member states in the early years, and several delegations complained that this made it impossible to assess whether each member state had fulfilled its obligations.[6]

The Debate

The debate over discriminatory QRs in the implementation phase generated the same pattern of alignment that had occurred during the accession negotiations. The meetings often degenerated into lengthy disputes about the extent to which the EC was abiding by, or reneging on, the commitments undertaken when the agreements were signed. While all three Eastern European countries argued that the EC failed to live up to the spirit of the protocols, the Hungarian delegation pursued the attack most vigorously. It consistently argued that the slow pace at which the Community was removing restrictions failed to comply with the obligations laid out in the agreement. Barring exceptional circumstances, the restrictions applied against Hungarian products should have been removed by January 1, 1975. The socialist countries received substantial vocal support from other delegations, including the United States, Canada, Australia, and Japan.

The EC resolutely maintained that it was indeed fulfilling the obligations imposed by the agreements. The Community's representative, when defending what he at times admitted was a slow pace of liberalization, pointed to systemic economic differences as obstacles to the removal of the discriminatory QRs. He stressed that the system of price formation in nonmarket countries justified maintaining discriminatory QRs, because many of the products exported from Eastern Europe could be heavily subsidized and would thus pose an excessive threat to domestic producers of similar products in Western Europe. When referring to the "exceptional reasons" required to justify QRs that were maintained against Hungarian products after the deadline of January 1975, the Community's representative pointed to the economic situation of recession in Western Europe. He spoke about increasing unemployment rates and reduced exports in 1975, the difficult economic situation in 1977, the exceptional economic situation prevailing in 1979, the economic crisis in 1981, and the difficult economic conditions in 1983.

These arguments were received with much skepticism from many quarters, getting a strong rebuttal from the Eastern European delegations and from representatives of other countries, including the United States, Canada, Australia, and Japan. They all made it clear that their governments wanted the discriminatory QRs removed in accordance with the terms of agreement, and they dismissed the Community's trade policy concerns as irrelevant. The opponents of the discriminatory QRs pointed out that there was an ample supply of other, more appropriate, multilateral safeguard mechanisms available for restricting imports should there be a threat of market disruption. Articles 6 and 19 of the General Agreement were specifically designed to protect domestic producers from market disruption. Moreover, a special discriminatory safeguard clause had been inserted into the protocols of accession to accommodate the Community's trade policy concerns. The Hungarian representative also suggested that the Community was setting a dangerous precedent for the General Agreement as a whole by citing the economic recession as a reason for waiving obligations. Citing the economic recession as a reason for restricting the imports from Hungary was not convincing because it failed to explain why imports of similar products from other contracting parties were not likewise restricted.[7]

Despite this opposition, the EC continued to maintain a number of discriminatory QRs against Rumanian and Hungarian products long after the target dates for elimination that had been inserted into these two countries' protocols of accession to the GATT. For example, according to the Rumanian representative, in 1980 the Community still applied discriminatory restrictions against approximately 8 percent of its imports from Rumania.[8]

Although some discriminatory QRs were applied throughout the 1980s, the commercial stakes were not very significant. To explain the intensity of the dispute, one has to turn to issues of principle and to broader trade policy debates. The Hungarian delegation's energetic and persistent attempts to remove the discriminatory QRs stemmed largely from matters of principle and a determination to eliminate discriminatory trade practices generally. Hungary was under no grand illusions that it would reap substantial commercial benefits through the elimination of the remaining discriminatory QRs.[9] From 4 to 6.5 percent of Hungarian exports to the EC in 1985 were affected by the QRs,[10] but at least 20 percent of the QRs applied in the late 1980s covered products that were not even produced in Hungary and therefore had no effect on Hungarian trade.[11] A much more substantive issue of concern was the Community's common agricultural policy, which acted as a far greater impediment to Hungarian exports than did the discriminatory QRs. In the late 1980s agricultural

products made up 30 percent of Hungary's total exports of mer-
chandise to convertible currency areas, and according to Hungarian
estimates the damage to its agriculture arising from protectionism
and subsidies in developed market economies was between $150
million and $200 million annually.[12]

Those governments, including the United States, that supported
the socialist countries during the meetings had negligible commercial
interests at stake in the dispute. They likewise opposed the Community's position as a matter of principle. As one American official
explained, "If the Community breaks its obligations, that weakens
the entire system. The Community didn't live up to its obligations.
We're not going to go to bat to help a nonmarket economy country,
but the principle is still important."[13]

Constraints against Implementation

The EC was placed under increasing pressure to remove the QRs
during the 1980s because of several developments.[14] First, the EC
representative became the only defender of QRs during the reviews
of the Hungarian protocol after Sweden and Norway eliminated their
discriminatory QRs vis-à-vis Hungary in 1982 and 1984, respectively.[15] Second, representatives from other governments, especially
the United States, Canada, Australia, and Japan, became increasingly
vocal during the meetings and clearly expressed their growing im-
patience with the EC for its failure to eliminate the discriminatory
import regulations.[16] Finally, the EC was placed in a more vulnerable
position when the focus of the debate partly shifted to the less
ambiguously phrased part of the agreement, which stated, "Contracting parties . . . shall not increase the discriminatory element in
these restrictions." The Community's record on compliance with this
part of the agreement became the subject of much dispute when
Greece acceded to the EC and when general quotas applied by the
EC against a broader range of countries were removed for all market
economy GATT members. This left the nonmarket countries the only
ones against which these quotas were imposed. In short, quotas that
were previously nondiscriminatory became discriminatory.[17]

Yet this growing pressure failed to have any significant impact on
the EC because it was counteracted by other factors. The general
attitude of GATT members toward the Eastern European countries
undermined the pressure placed on the Community during the pe-

riodic meetings. The tendency of GATT members is to take a different approach toward nonmarket countries. The potential for damage to the reputations of members reneging on an agreement is therefore substantially lessened if the agreement is with a nonmarket country.[18] As one Western official stated, "The EC's nonfulfillment of the agreement has had no practical value simply because Eastern European countries are thought of as second-class citizens in the GATT. They have no standing."[19] Furthermore, the incentive for the Western European countries to remove the QRs in order to maintain a creditworthy reputation was undermined by the fact that the Commission, rather than the EC countries themselves, had to defend the EC position in the GATT forum and take the brunt of the attacks during the biennial meetings. However, the power to remove the QRs lay with the member states, not the Commission. The EC states thus used the Commission as a "smokescreen."[20] As one official from an EC country explained, "We experience no feeling of embarrassment in the GATT as it's the Commission that takes the embarrassment. The member countries just sit quietly in the reviews and let the Commission take the brunt."[21]

In short, for many years the pressure exerted in the GATT forum was insufficient to induce the EC to bring its trade practices into conformity with GATT regulations. It required a sharp change in broader political considerations to do so. As will be discussed later in this chapter, developments in the political arena in the late 1980s provided the necessary precondition for resolving the long-standing trade policy dispute over discriminatory QRs.

Bilateralism versus Multilateralism

The negotiations during the implementation stage at times became entangled in transatlantic disputes that had little to do with East-West relations, but were part of a broader trade policy conflict between the United States and the EC over bilateralism versus multilateralism. Discriminatory QRs was not the only issue that triggered this broader debate. Bilateral trade agreements that were being negotiated between the Community and certain Eastern European countries in the 1980s were also important. The subject of preferential, or discriminatory, bilateral agreements had long been a source of transatlantic conflict and, like discriminatory QRs, had plagued the negotiations over the International Trade Organization in the 1940s. At that time, the United States fought to eliminate such preferential or discriminatory trade agreements as the British imperial preference system. The issue had likewise surfaced as a major source of conflict when the EC negotiated numerous preferential trade agreements—for example, those reached with the Mediterranean countries—that denied the United States the nondiscriminatory treatment (or equal market access) associated with the unconditional MFN clause and GATT membership.

The transatlantic disputes over preferential trade agreements first arose in the context of negotiations with the East when the Community concluded a bilateral agreement with Rumania in 1980. The terms of this bilateral trade agreement included one clause that could have undermined the GATT norm of nondiscrimination. It thus elicited a fairly negative reaction from the U.S. and Canadian governments, whose delegations to the GATT raised the issue during one of the periodic meetings designed to oversee the implementation of the Rumanian protocol of accession. The controversy centered on the ninth clause of the bilateral agreement, which stated, "Romania will expand and diversify its imports of products originating in the Community at a rate not smaller than its purchases from the other Contracting Parties to the GATT."[22]

American trade policy officials were concerned that this clause might grant the Community preferential access to the Rumanian market, harm American exporters, and undermine the norm of nondiscrimination. The American desire to uphold nondiscrimination in this case, and in later negotiations for bilateral agreements between the EC and other Eastern European countries, was heightened by a broader determination to halt what many American officials perceived to be a "proliferation of the Community's preferential agreements."[23] As one American official stated, "Ever since the founding of the Community we've had problems with their special regional preferences. It's an issue of U.S. multilateralism versus EC regionalism."[24] Another official explained that the United States believed that the agreements "should be nondiscriminatory. It's a matter of principle. There are also small trade interests, but it's a matter of principle."[25]

The third biennial review of Rumania's multilateral agreement with the GATT, held in 1980, provided the American and Canadian delegations with an opportunity to express their concern about the ninth clause. The delegations worried that the bilateral agreement was not in full conformity with the multilateral GATT rules on non-discrimination and might grant the Community preferential access to the Rumanian market. These fears were viewed as unfounded by the Rumanian and Community representatives, who insisted that the agreement was neither a preferential nor a market-sharing agreement but was based on trade competitiveness. They assured the concerned parties that the agreement would be implemented in compliance with GATT provisions and in compliance with the provisions of Rumania's protocol of accession to the GATT.[26]

The incident passed without further drama, but it nonetheless served as a reminder that the subject of Soviet and Eastern European participation in the international trading system ties into a far broader trade policy debate that has little to do with Eastern Europe per se. The subject is part of the larger question of how to maintain an integrated global economy and prevent a further proliferation of discriminatory trade practices that could move the world back to the 1930s. The postwar planners concluded that a universal trading institution was the best route for pursuing this goal, and it may well be argued today that the integration of the former Soviet Union and Eastern Europe into the GATT should be encouraged in order to advance the broader goal of multilateralism. Inclusion in the GATT provides a forum for opposing the development of bilateralism in trade relations with the East.

Entrance Fees

While sharing some important common features, the protocols of accession reached with Poland, Rumania, and Hungary imposed different obligations on each country. The variation in the entrance fees meant that the periodic reviews of the individual agreements, which evaluated the extent to which the Eastern European countries were meeting their commitments, focused on different questions.

In the Polish case the review assessed whether Poland was fulfilling its commitment to increase imports from contracting parties by 7 percent annually. The issue caused some dispute in the 1968 meeting, and the working party noted that Poland had only increased imports from GATT countries by 6 percent. However, in all other years of the first decade of GATT membership, Poland not only fulfilled its obligation but also surpassed the 7 percent target. Polish imports from contracting parties increased by 9.3 percent in 1969; 7.9 percent in 1970; 18 percent in 1971; 48.9 percent in 1972; 65.3 percent in 1973; 41.8 percent in 1974; 15.1 percent in 1975; and 11.4 percent in 1976.[27] This outstanding record was no doubt helped by the large credits that Poland received during this period. It is also very possible that the Polish commitment in the GATT forum was an irrelevant factor and had no influence over Polish import decisions.

Poland's record changed in 1977, when it failed to fulfill its commitment to increase imports by 7 percent. The reviews of the Polish protocol of accession were subsequently suspended to allow some informal discussions about revising the terms of Poland's obligation. But the informal discussions led to no agreement, and the annual consultations were not resumed.[28]

The Rumanian entrance fee did not include the very specific commitment undertaken by Poland. Rumania agreed to intend firmly to increase its imports from contracting parties at a rate not smaller than the growth of total Rumanian imports provided for in its five-year plans. But the precise obligations imposed on Rumania were somewhat ambiguous because the accord only referred to planned imports and said nothing about actual imports. The reports of the meetings held in 1977 and 1980 stated that the working parties noted that Rumania had fulfilled its import commitment.[29] Similar conclusions were not included in the reports of subsequent meetings. Instead, by the mid-1980s representatives from several countries began to question whether Rumania had indeed fulfilled its obligations. The Canadian and Community representatives considered the data provided by the Rumanian delegation in the mid-1980s inadequate. They argued that this lack of information from the Rumanian government was a failure to comply with the obligations of GATT membership. Representatives from other countries, including Sweden and the United States, also began to question whether Rumania was complying with its import commitment. A fair amount of attention was devoted to this issue in the 1987 meeting because actual Rumanian imports from contracting parties had declined at a greater rate than the total decline of Rumanian imports in 1986.[30]

The specific obligations imposed on Hungary were very different from the quantitative commitments undertaken by Poland and Rumania. Hungary's obligation was that it, like any other contracting party, was required to keep tariff levels at the rates agreed upon during the course of negotiations. Thus the meetings that were held to review the Hungarian protocol did not directly consider the entrance fee, but instead reviewed the development of Hungarian imports and foreign trade regulations. One of the objectives of this examination was to ensure that Hungary abide by its commitment that trade regulations applied to socialist countries would not operate to the detriment of contracting parties. Some members of the working parties accordingly posed questions on the development of Hungarian imports and foreign trade regulations during the second part of the biennial meetings.[31]

There appears to be a general consensus among GATT members that the experience of the implementation stage indicates that none of the entrance fees were totally satisfactory mechanisms for obtaining reciprocity from nonmarket countries upon accession to the GATT. It is extremely difficult, if not impossible, to obtain evidence that would indicate whether contracting parties did indeed obtain increased export opportunities as a result of these entrance fees or whether export opportunities would have been the same regardless of the Eastern European commitments to the GATT. Nevertheless, many observers consider that the commitments undertaken by the nonmarket countries had little impact on the development of trade.

The socialist countries, in turn, received few tangible benefits upon accession to the GATT. Membership provided them with little in the way of increased access to Western markets, although this had been an important objective for the Eastern countries when they first approached the GATT. The United States extended MFN treatment to Polish products in 1960, before Poland's accession, and then withdrew this favorable treatment in the early 1980s when martial law was imposed; and the United States invoked article 35 of the GATT when Rumania and Hungary joined the international trade institution. The EC failed to remove all the discriminatory QRs applied against products from the East and of course retained other general protectionist measures such as the common agricultural policy.

The Post-Cold-War World

The new realities of the post-cold-war world pose the task of normalizing the terms of participation for those Eastern countries that are already members of the GATT. Some steps toward this goal had been taken by mid-1991, but much remained to be done. The most significant developments, which occurred at the end of the 1980s, centered on the resolution of the long-standing disputes over discriminatory QRs. Favorable political circumstances acted as a significant impetus for resolving a trade policy problem that appeared unresolvable under less favorable political conditions.

The specific political issues that induced the EC states to change their position in the late 1980s grew out of specific problems that had long plagued bilateral relations between the European Community and Eastern Europe.

The Soviet Union had adopted a hostile approach toward the European Community when it was first created. This hostility was significantly reduced during the 1960s, but relations between the Council for Mutual Economic Assistance (CMEA) and the EC remained problematic for many years. The Community had sought to normalize relations with the East through the conclusion of bilateral trade agreements with individual Eastern European countries, as it had done with most other countries in the world in the 1960s when the authority to conclude trade agreements was transferred from the individual EC states to the Community. However, the CMEA had opposed the negotiation of bilateral trade agreements between the EC and individual Eastern European countries. Instead, it favored the negotiation of a bilateral trade agreement between the EC and the CMEA, leaving only technical matters as a subject for agreements between the Community and individual Eastern countries. The lengthy dispute over appropriate signatories to trade agreements had left a vacuum in relations between the EC and Eastern Europe. No legal framework existed to guide the conduct of trade.[32] Rumania alone had entered into a bilateral trade agreement with the Community.[33]

The CMEA changed its position toward the question of appropriate signatories in the mid-1980s and thus opened the path to a normalization of relations with the EC. The new CMEA position, more in line with the Community's approach, proposed that official relations be established between the two organizations through the adoption of a joint declaration, while bilateral trade agreements were concluded between the Community and individual Eastern European countries. The Community in turn adopted what became known as the parallel approach: the EC would enter into negotiations for a joint declaration with the CMEA but would simultaneously enter into negotiations for the normalization of relations with individual CMEA states. These broader developments set the context for understanding the resolution of the EC-Hungarian conflict over discriminatory QRs.

Discriminatory QRs

The Hungarian government had begun negotiations for a bilateral trade agreement with the Community in the early 1980s, before the change in the CMEA's position. But these negotiations broke down in 1983 and 1984. One of the stumbling blocks to agreement had been the EC states' unwillingness to agree to the Hungarian demand that a bilateral agreement clearly require the elimination of discriminatory QRs in conformity with the Community's obligations under Hungary's multilateral agreement with the GATT.[34] The bilateral negotiations were resumed in 1986 and accelerated rapidly in the spring of 1988. At that time, the EC states finally agreed to the Hungarian demand that the terms of a bilateral trade agreement unambiguously require the removal of remaining discriminatory restrictions.[35]

The EC's unprecedented concession toward Hungary in the spring of 1988 is explained by several factors. These generated a strong desire to reach an agreement with Hungary at that time, leaving the EC members with no alternative but to accept the Hungarian demand that the terms of agreement eliminate discriminatory QRs. First, the Community's stated objective since the outset of the EC-CMEA negotiations had been to conclude bilateral trade agreements with individual Eastern European countries parallel with the signing of the Joint Declaration. It was evident in the spring of 1988 that the negotiations for the EC-CMEA Joint Declaration would be shortly concluded. Thus the political incentive to reach an agreement was heightened.[36] Second, Hungary's generally good image in the West led many members of the Community to believe it should be among the first of the Eastern European countries to conclude an agreement with the EC.[37] Finally, the pressure to reach an agreement was intensified by the impending conclusion of West Germany's presidency of the Community at the end of June 1988. Improved relations with the East had apparently been one of the major goals that West Germany had set out to fulfil during its six-month term in the rotating presidency. German officials therefore adopted a particularly active and constructive approach during the negotiations with Hungary.[38]

The EC-Hungarian bilateral trade and cooperation agreement was initialed on June 30, 1988, several days after the signing of the Joint Declaration. Among other issues, the trade agreement provided for a three-phase removal of the discriminatory quantitative restrictions, with those against "non-sensitive products," "fairly sensitive products," and "highly sensitive products" to be eliminated in 1989, 1992, and 1995, respectively. The agreement also included a special safeguard mechanism providing an accelerated procedure for restricting imports of "highly sensitive products" between 1995 and 1998.[39]

After the signing of the agreement, political circumstances changed again and induced another shift in the EC's position toward the remaining discriminatory QRs. This time two countries were singled out for the favorable economic treatment that was granted as part of twenty-four Western countries' (the "Group of 24") special program, commonly known as PHARE, to help Poland and Hungary to restructure their economies. In early November 1989, in the context of PHARE, the EC decided to remove all remaining discriminatory QRs applied against Polish and Hungarian products by January 1990. Similar treatment was then extended to Czechoslovakia and Bulgaria in October 1990.[40]

The change in the Community's position toward discriminatory QRs provides some grounds for optimism about resolving the trade policy problems caused by nonmarket countries' participation in the GATT in the future. The Community's decision to remove the discriminatory restrictions appears to have been driven by political rather than economic considerations. Poland and Hungary had barely embarked on the long and difficult road of economic reform when the restrictions were removed. This indicates that the trade policy problems posed by nonmarket countries may in fact not present the insurmountable barriers that they were portrayed to present in the past.

Normalizing Relations with the GATT

By mid-1991 Western governments had embarked on the task of adjusting to the post-cold-war world, making changes in their policies toward trade with the East. Progress had been most notable in bilateral relations. The EC concluded bilateral trade and cooperation agreements with the individual Eastern European countries by October 1990. The EC was involved in negotiating association agreements with Poland, Hungary, and Czechoslovakia. Substantial problems were encountered, however, because of the EC states' unwillingness to grant significantly increased market access in the key sectors of interest to the Eastern countries—agriculture, textiles, and steel. U.S. trade policy officials, in line with their traditional desire to avoid a proliferation of the EC's preferential trade agreements, have carefully followed the EC's negotiations for bilateral trade and cooperation agreements with the Eastern countries. History indicates that American trade policy officials will also take an active interest in the EC's association agreements, which will have to be submitted for review in the GATT forum in accordance with article 24 of the General Agreement. The United States has itself concluded bilateral trade agreements with the Eastern countries, the terms of which are in full conformity with the GATT.[41]

There have also been some signs of change in the multilateral arena, but the task of fully integrating Poland, Hungary, and Rumania into the GATT remained incomplete by mid-1991. The second-class citizenship terms of participation for these countries were drawn up in an era very different from that which exists today. The dramatic changes in the East have now placed the subject of normalization onto the agenda for the post-cold-war world.

The normalizing discussions formally began early in 1990, when the Polish government submitted a formal request to renegotiate the terms of its participation in the GATT. A working party was promptly established in February 1990 to examine Poland's request to renegotiate its terms of accession to the GATT.[42] The Hungarian government has likewise expressed a desire to change its terms of participation in the GATT, although this request did not come until the spring of 1991, and little concrete action had been taken by the summer of that year.[43] The Rumanian government has said that it is not yet ready to renegotiate its protocol of accession and that it would take some time before progress on economic reform is advanced enough for Rumania to formally apply for a change in the terms of its participation.

The procedures being used to renegotiate the Polish protocol of accession are similar to those used when Poland first applied to join the GATT. The Polish government was asked to submit a memorandum on its foreign trade regime. Contracting parties were invited to pose written questions on the memorandum, and the Polish government was then given the opportunity to provide written responses to those questions. This process took well over a year to complete, and the first meeting of the working party was held in July 1991.

Poland and Hungary are both asking that their terms of participation in the GATT be the same as those accorded to market economy countries. This would mean that all the unusual clauses inserted into the original agreements would be excluded from the new agreements. These include the discriminatory safeguard clause, the clause on discriminatory QRs (which is no longer relevant because the discriminatory QRs have been removed), and the provisions for periodic reviews. In addition, the Polish government has requested that its entrance fee, a quantitative commitment, be replaced by the conventional procedure of tariff negotiations.[44]

Finally, the Hungarian and Rumanian governments have pressed their long-standing requests that the United States disinvoke article 35 of the GATT, which provides for the nonapplication of the General Agreement between two members, in order to normalize these countries' situation in the international trading system.[45] The United States has made moves to this end. The route chosen by the Bush administration is not to change the legislation that requires the United States to invoke article 35. Instead, the administration plans to allow certain countries to "graduate" from the provisions of title IV of the 1974 Trade Act. A bill is currently pending in Congress that would permit terminating the application of title IV for Hungary and Czechoslovakia, thus enabling the United States to grant these two countries permanent MFN status and to disinvoke article 35 of the GATT.[46]

In short, the West is now faced with the task of renegotiating the terms of participation for the former socialist countries that are already members of the GATT. Other very important subjects on the agenda for the post-cold-war era will now be broached as I turn to the negotiations regarding Bulgarian and Soviet bids to affiliate with the GATT.

Chapter 5

Bulgaria's Bid to Join the GATT

THE COLLAPSE OF Soviet control over Eastern Europe has opened the path to the resolution of many conflicts in East-West relations, including some that concern Eastern participation in the international trading system. The end of the cold war has changed the agenda for negotiations over Eastern countries' relations with the GATT. Current challenges include developing an appropriate policy toward applications from Bulgaria and the Soviet Union's successor states, Eastern countries that are not yet members of the international trade institution.

Bulgaria has been trying to increase its affiliation with the GATT for many years, with little success. An analysis of the past negotiations with Bulgaria indicates that its ability to join the GATT in the future will depend not only on economic developments in that country but also on a fundamental restructuring of Western policies in light of the new political realities of the post-cold-war world.

Initial Approaches, 1970s

The affiliation of Bulgaria with the GATT dates to June 1967, when it applied for observer status. The conventional institutional practice at that time was to automatically grant observer status to any country that submitted a request, and the application was accordingly approved at a council meeting on June 26, 1967.[1]

Bulgaria made some further efforts to increase its participation in the GATT in the 1970s, but the approaches were informal and not extensive. The requests at that time drew on the Hungarian precedent and focused on accession to full membership through the conventional procedure of tariff concessions.[2] Bulgaria's request, although not bluntly rebuffed, was not greeted with enthusiasm. The country was not given the encouragement that had been extended to Poland, Rumania, and Hungary under the policy of differentiation.[3] The request apparently elicited a particularly unenthusiastic response from the Commission of the European Communities in 1980, providing the first signs of the more extreme hostility that was to emerge between the Commission and Bulgaria in the next few years.[4]

The Commission's negative position resulted from a variety of considerations. The stated reason was that reciprocity would not be obtained should Bulgaria merely grant tariff concessions as an entrance fee. While reciprocity was indeed an important consideration for the Community, as it had been in negotiations with the other nonmarket countries, it was not the only factor at work.[5] There was also some concern that negotiations in the GATT forum might undermine the Community's broader policy toward the East, which aimed to induce individual Eastern European countries to break ranks with CMEA policy and normalize relations with the Community through the conclusion of bilateral trade agreements. Commission officials thought that accession to the GATT had made it easier for Poland and Hungary to avoid negotiating a bilateral trade agreement with the Community and that the same would happen with Bulgaria should it join the GATT. Membership in the GATT would provide Bulgaria with a legal framework for conducting trade with the EC and would entitle Bulgaria to de jure MFN status, thus leaving Bulgaria with no incentive to conclude a bilateral agreement. Furthermore, membership in the GATT would provide Bulgaria with an opportunity to join the other socialist countries in their fight against certain aspects of the Community's commercial policy, such as discriminatory quantitative restrictions. Finally, there was already some concern by the late 1970s that an agreement between Bulgaria and the GATT might set an undesirable precedent for the Soviet Union.[6]

Nothing of substance emerged from these informal discussions at the end of the 1970s. The Bulgarian government did not push its demands any further, and the subject was put aside without much drama. Subsequent negotiations between Bulgaria and the GATT were to proceed far less quietly. Many obstacles were encountered as the Bulgarian case became increasingly enmeshed in the Soviet case.

The factors driving the negotiations with Bulgaria in the 1980s, to which I now turn, were in many ways similar to the Polish, Rumanian, and Hungarian cases. Political issues were once again a very important consideration. However, in the Bulgarian case the West's strategic objectives dictated conflict rather than cooperation. Bulgarian requests were therefore blocked at times without any serious consideration of how to resolve the trade policy dilemmas. On those occasions when trade policy issues did surface as a real concern, the negotiations once again became caught up in broader transatlantic conflicts over nondiscrimination.

The Standards Code

The Bulgarian strategy shifted in the early 1980s. The idea of full accession to the GATT was placed aside, and the government instead focused on accession to the arrangements and codes that had been drawn up during the Tokyo Round. Bulgaria encountered no obstacles when it joined the Arrangement Regarding Bovine Meat and the International Dairy Arrangement in January 1980. Participation in these arrangements was open to all members of the United Nations. There were no conditions for accession, because the arrangements imposed no significant obligations. The main commitments were merely that signatories provide data and information that would facilitate monitoring the overall situation for the world market in these products.[7]

The problems began when Bulgaria expressed an interest in joining the standards code. This code (officially known as the Agreement on Technical Barriers to Trade) had been drawn up to ensure that national standards designed to protect, for example, health, safety, and the environment did not act as barriers to trade. The standards code, like the other codes that had been established during the Tokyo Round, involved more substantive commitments than the arrangements. Thus the subject of accession to the codes was more complex. A declaration by the GATT Trade Negotiations Committee in April 1979 had stated that countries that were not members of the GATT were eligible to join the codes after negotiations. These negotiations would aim to secure an overall parity of rights and obligations between two groups of countries: signatories to the codes that were contracting parties to the GATT and signatories that were not. It was subsequently agreed that the precise terms of accession for noncontracting parties would be dealt with by each code's committee on an ad hoc basis.[8]

Bulgaria notified the chair of the standards code's committee on July 10, 1980, that it wanted to start negotiations for accession to the code.[9] Bulgarian officials had apparently chosen this specific code because they thought it presented a most likely case for successful agreement. The standards code was more technical than other codes, and there was no particular reason why a country with a planned economy could not comply with the code's commitments.[10]

Ironically, Bulgaria's highly centralized system was in some respects particularly suited for undertaking the code's obligations, which included avoiding the use of standards as a barrier to trade, accepting the results of international testing and certification procedures, accepting international standards as a basis for domestic regulations, and increasing the provision of information on national standards for foreign producers.[11] When the code was drawn up there had been substantial dispute over the potential imbalance of obligations that would accrue to countries with more centralized political systems. The EC had consistently argued that countries with federal systems of government (such as the United States) would not assume as many obligations as countries with unified political systems where technical regulations are adopted by the national government. A federal government could not ensure full compliance with the code because much of the relevant legislation would be drawn up at the subnational or regional level. The regional units would not be legally bound to abide by an international code signed by the national government.[12] Thus Bulgaria, with its highly centralized system, would fall into the category of countries that could assume greater obligations.

In view of this, Bulgaria could expect to encounter few technical problems when applying to join the standards code. Nonetheless, numerous obstacles were encountered; and, in the words of one Western official, "technical counterarguments [were] put forward for what [were] really far more important reasons."[13] The negotiations initially proceeded with a fair degree of regularity, despite constant opposition from the EC Commission. However, by mid-1981 the Bulgarian application was clearly a lost cause owing to a U.S. shift to extreme hostility. The Bulgarian case became completely enmeshed with the Soviet case in the eyes of many American officials, and the new cold war of the early 1980s dictated opposing any agreements that might set a precedent for Soviet affiliation with the GATT.

Trade Policy Issues, 1980–81

The Bulgarian application to join the standards code initially received a relatively neutral response from the United States in the early fall of 1980. The American position was not heavily influenced by broader political considerations at this early stage, and although Bulgaria did not receive the support extended to Poland, Rumania, and Hungary, it was also not bluntly opposed. The United States did, however, want a thorough examination of trade policy issues because it had some concern that even if Bulgaria's technical standards should conform with the code's rules, these measures could be undermined by other regulations used to control imports. The United States therefore proposed that a working party be established to examine these trade policy questions.[14]

The American proposal was accepted despite sharp opposition from the Bulgarian representative, who considered that such a thorough review would constitute discrimination. He argued that other members of the code had not been submitted to this kind of examination.[15] The working party's terms of reference were "to draw up proposals for mutually satisfactory terms for the accession of Bulgaria to the Agreement on Technical Barriers to Trade and to report to the Committee prior to the next meeting."[16]

At this stage intra-Community and transatlantic differences began to emerge, creating a fair degree of confusion that was to last for several years. First, different interests and positions within the EC often impeded the development of a coherent common position. Second, the differences within the West were initially heightened by broader transatlantic disputes over trade policy issues that were brought out by the Bulgarian case. The divergent transatlantic approaches became reconciled by mid-1981, when the American government abandoned any concern for trade policy issues and became submerged in the broader political issues at stake. However, the confusion continued because of the persistent differences within the EC and the emergence of a "cat-and-mouse" game between the United States and the Community.

The EC Commission adopted a particularly firm position from the outset. There was substantial concern that Bulgaria's request to join the standards code might be part of what was termed a creeping accession policy. Some officials feared that Bulgaria might be pursuing a strategy that would enable it to increase its affiliation with the GATT through the "back door" by joining codes and evading regular accession procedures under article 33 of the General Agreement.[17] This was regarded as extremely undesirable because of a growing fear of creating a precedent for the Soviet Union.[18] Soviet officials had tentatively begun to express some interest in affiliation with the GATT by that time. The EC Commission and some of the EC states therefore advocated very tough conditions for Bulgaria's accession to the standards code.

The somewhat harsh approach that was adopted by certain elements of the Community initially received little support from the United States, which maintained a more neutral stance throughout the first half of 1981. The United States "welcomed" the Bulgarian application, but desired a thorough examination of trade policy issues.

This lack of support from the United States left the Community's representative totally isolated in his tough stance toward Bulgaria. This isolation was evident at a working party meeting held to discuss the subject in March 1981. At this meeting the American, Canadian, and Community representatives all questioned the Bulgarian representative on relevant aspects of his country's regulations. The Swiss, Japanese, and Nordic representatives remained silent throughout. The detailed and lengthy responses given by the Bulgarian representative were generally viewed as satisfactory by all members of the working party, with the apparent exception of the Community.[19] The Community's representative then continued to ask further questions about the Bulgarian system. He received no support from either the American or the Canadian representatives.[20]

The Community representative's position at this March meeting was made even more awkward by the fact that he did not have the support of all the EC states. Thus he was not able to announce the EC's proposal for the terms of Bulgaria's accession to the standards code. The Community was in the process of considering a proposal, but West Germany had requested that no move be made in the GATT forum until further discussions were held in an internal Community meeting in Brussels. When the discussion in the working party meeting turned to the question of possible terms of accession, the EC representative was therefore merely able to announce that the draft terms for noncontracting parties' accession to the codes that had been stated by the Trade Negotiations Committee in April 1979 would be inadequate for this case. This statement received no vocal support from any other representatives present at the meeting.[21]

The Community's proposal for the terms of Bulgaria's accession to the standards code became public the following month. The proposal included the insertion of a special discriminatory safeguard clause that would act as a substitute for, or permit evasion of, the code's multilateral dispute settlement procedure. Signatories that were contracting parties to the GATT would be able to take unilateral action and withdraw obligations vis-à-vis Bulgaria should a dispute arise.

The EC's official justification for proposing this discriminatory clause omitted any reference to the fear of creating a precedent for the Soviet Union and focused exclusively on trade policy issues. It was argued that Bulgaria, as a noncontracting party to the GATT, did not have the same obligations as signatories to the code that were contracting parties to the GATT, because Bulgaria was not bound to respect broader rules of the General Agreement. Thus a potential imbalance of obligations could arise. Any signatory that considered it had been injured owing to the lack of broader obligations on Bulgaria's part should have the ability to take measures that would correct the unbalanced situation.[22] In short, the EC maintained that reciprocity would not be upheld even if Bulgaria should comply with the obligations of the code, because Bulgaria was not bound to comply with other GATT rules. This problem of ensuring reciprocity was said to justify a departure from the norm of nondiscrimination.

The proposal to insert a discriminatory safeguard clause into the agreement was strongly opposed by Bulgaria. It also generated opposition from others as the subject became entangled in larger debates over multilateralism. The Community's proposal received no support from other contracting parties during the late spring of 1981. The United States, Canada, the Nordic countries, and Switzerland indicated they were hesitant to include a clause that would permit an evasion of the code's multilateral dispute settlement procedures.[23]

The American reservations about the EC's proposal were influenced by a desire to uphold multilateralism. Some American officials apparently opposed setting a precedent that would provide a way to evade the code's multilateral dispute settlement procedure. It seems that their primary concern was to maintain the integrity of the standards code even if this meant granting Bulgaria less harsh terms of accession that might not fully uphold reciprocity. The American government decided to play a passive role and take a back seat at this stage. It made clear that the United States would accept any terms acceptable to the Community and Bulgaria providing that the terms of the agreement would not harm the standards code.[24]

The situation was in some ways similar to the negotiations with Poland, Rumania, and Hungary. During those negotiations, the Community's discriminatory QRs had also caused many problems, triggering the reemergence of the long-standing transatlantic dispute over quantitative restrictions. Although the West-West differences in the negotiations with Bulgaria were less intense than those over the subject of discriminatory QRs, the opposing transatlantic positions likewise reflected a broader dispute. The different transatlantic positions on a discriminatory safeguard clause for Bulgaria reflected a larger EC-U.S. dispute that had prevailed in the 1970s, when an attempt had been made to revise the main safeguard clause embodied in article 19 of the General Agreement. These earlier negotiations in the Tokyo Round were a failure. One of the main obstacles to agreement had been the EC's insistence that the new safeguard clause allow for selective or discriminatory measures. The United States, in contrast, had usually supported the developing countries in their attempts to ensure that a new safeguard clause for the General Agreement retain the traditional nondiscriminatory approach.[25]

Not only was the Community's proposal to include a special discriminatory safeguard clause in the agreement with Bulgaria opposed by other delegations, it even lacked full support from the EC's own members. It was favored by France, Italy, and Belgium. But some other countries, particularly West Germany, had certain reservations that were clearly evident by May 1981.[26] The German position was consistent with its generally more forthcoming attitude toward negotiations with Bulgaria in the GATT forum and stemmed from its broader political objectives in the East. As noted in chapter 2, West Germany's Ostpolitik was one of synchronization rather than differentiation. Bulgaria was not to be denied the supportive treatment extended to Poland, Rumania, and Hungary. The policy of synchronization spilled over into these negotiations in the GATT forum and apparently contributed to the more forthcoming position adopted toward Bulgaria. In addition, it appears that West Germany considered it inappropriate for the Community to maintain an isolated position,[27] and argued that Bulgaria's centralized political system made it particularly suited for adhering to the code's obligations.[28]

Political-Security Issues and the New Cold War

The divergent transatlantic positions toward possible terms for Bulgaria's accession to the standards code were evident until the end of May 1981. The Community's position was isolated in the GATT forum, and even several of its own member states lacked enthusiasm for it.[29] This situation began to change in June 1981, when the United States abandoned its previous position. By early July the United States opposed Bulgarian participation in the GATT. It supported the Community's proposal to include a special discriminatory safeguard clause even if this permitted evasion of the standards code's multilateral dispute settlement procedure.[30]

The United States was to remain fundamentally opposed to Bulgarian participation throughout the decade. Bulgaria was viewed as a stalking horse for the Soviet Union. Bulgaria's participation in the GATT was to be resisted in order to avoid creating a precedent for the USSR.[31] In short, the Bulgarian case had become entirely enmeshed in the Soviet case.

The American policy reversal was caused by several interrelated factors. The shift was apparently triggered when Commission officials increased their efforts to obtain American support. The Community's difficulties in maintaining an isolated position in the GATT forum had become particularly obvious at a working party meeting held on June 10, 1981. It seems that Commission officials subsequently managed to raise the issue to a higher level in the U.S. government and bring the matter to the attention of key American officials.[32]

The more important cause for the Community's success in obtaining American support stemmed from the underlying shift in the Reagan administration's position toward trade with the East.[33] Many officials in the Reagan administration adopted a hard-line position. They were shortly to embark on their (unsuccessful) efforts to persuade, induce, and force Western European governments to do the same and to forgo the Urengoi Pipeline agreement. It seems that when the subject of Bulgaria and the GATT was brought to the attention of newly appointed prominent officials in the administration, political issues concerning security helped make them very amenable to cooperation with the Community, and to conflict with Bulgaria.[34] These issues led the United States to adopt a very negative approach toward trade with the Soviet Union and its closest allies, an approach that filtered through into the negotiations in the GATT forum and overwhelmed any previous desire to uphold multilateralism. The broader political constraints against cooperation with Bulgaria were to remain intact until the end of the 1980s.

The United States agreed to the Community's proposed terms for Bulgaria's accession to the standards code. However, the United States continued to play a fairly passive role, delegating the task of active opposition to the Community. The United States began to play a cat-and-mouse game. Although their basic objectives were similar, the United States preferred to leave the "dirty work" to the European Community and "to take refuge behind it." Opposition to the Bulgarian application was not easy to admit in public, since the GATT is supposed to be concerned with trade issues rather than political-security issues. Because this opposition could not be clearly justified by trade policy arguments, the United States adopted a low profile, leaving the unpleasant work of active opposition to the EC. The United States expressed support for the Community's position whenever it became evident that the Community could not hold out on its own.[35]

Two further working party meetings were held in 1981 to discuss the terms of Bulgaria's accession to the standards code. In the meeting in July the participants discussed a draft proposal that had been circulated by the Community. The proposal included a key clause stating that signatories to the code that were contracting parties to the GATT could unilaterally withdraw obligations to Bulgaria should a dispute arise. The proposal allowed unilateral action before using the code's multilateral dispute settlement procedure. It stated:

> In the event of a dispute between Bulgaria and another Party to the Agreement, the provisions of Article 14, paragraphs 1–22, shall apply. During the procedures under the said provisions of Article 14 and without prejudice to them, the Party or Bulgaria may, in exceptional circumstances in which the balance of rights

and obligations under the Agreement cannot be preserved otherwise, take provisional action in order to suspend such obligations
under the Agreement which it deems necessary in the circumstances to preserve the balance of rights and obligations under
the Agreement. Any such action would be promptly notified to
the Committee on Technical Barriers to Trade.[36]

This proposal was strongly opposed by the Bulgarian representative, and the lengthy working party meeting failed to lead to an
agreement. The Bulgarian government presented a counterproposal
at the next meeting in October, but it was opposed by the Community. The counterproposal would not have allowed the same degree of freedom of unilateral action permitted in the Community's
proposal. The chair of the working party then suggested moving to
informal negotiations and only reconvening the working party should
agreement appear imminent.[37]

The subject of Bulgaria's accession to the standards code resurfaced in 1983. Bulgarian officials at that time conducted informal
meetings with the representatives from EC states rather than with
the Commission. This contributed to much confusion that at one
point nearly led to an agreement. The Bulgarian proposal discussed
in these informal meetings received a particularly favorable response
from West Germany.[38] The initiatives also received an encouraging
response from representatives of other EC states and the Community
delegation in Geneva. The subject was then discussed at an internal
Community meeting, held in Geneva at the beginning of December
1983. The Bulgarian proposal was apparently approved by the representatives of the EC states at this meeting, and Bulgaria's accession
to the standards code therefore seemed quite possible at that time.[39]

Officials at the Commission headquarters in Brussels continued
to firmly oppose an agreement on the basis of the proposal that had
been discussed in Geneva. But their growing isolation once again
made it very difficult to maintain a strong stance. Their position
became particularly vulnerable after the internal Community meeting
held in Geneva in December, when the member states' representatives had apparently approved the Bulgarian proposal. The precise
picture of the actions of the Community (and its constituent parts)
then became rather blurred, by all accounts. Apparently, Commission officials in Brussels once again asked American officials for more

support, strongly conveying the urgency of their request.[40] The request was granted. As in June 1981, American officials confirmed their support when the Commission asserted that it could no longer oppose the Bulgarian application alone. American officials made it clear in relevant meetings that they opposed agreement on the basis of the Bulgarian proposal.[41] Bulgaria's bid to join the standards code was barred.

Criteria for Participation in the Uruguay Round

It became evident during the summer of 1986 that the Bulgarian policy was shifting back to a focus on accession to full membership in the GATT. On September 8 the Bulgarian government submitted an official application to accede to the GATT as a developing country in the course of the Uruguay Round (through the provision of article 33).[42]

This application, which came shortly after the Soviet request to participate in the Uruguay Round, received a very negative response from both the United States and the EC. However, the General Agreement included no rules that could be used to block the Bulgarian request. Western officials therefore decided to draft extremely precise and strict criteria to determine a country's eligibility to participate in the Uruguay Round. These would also provide the West with technical arguments for denying applications that were undesirable for far more important security reasons.

The new rules were written specifically to bar Bulgaria and the USSR from participation, while allowing for Chinese participation.[43] The rules were incorporated into the ministerial declaration of September 25, 1986, which launched the Uruguay Round. They stated:

Negotiations will be open to:
(1) all contracting parties,
(2) countries having acceded provisionally,
(3) countries applying to the GATT on a *de facto* basis having announced, not later than 30 April 1987, their intention to accede to the GATT and to participate in the negotiations,
(4) countries that have already informed the CONTRACTING PARTIES, at a regular meeting of the Council of Representatives, of their intention to negotiate the terms of their membership as a

contracting party, and

(5) developing countries that have, by 30 April 1987, initiated procedures for accession to the GATT, with the intention of negotiating the terms of their accession during the course of the negotiations.[44]

These new rules marked a complete reversal of the rules on eligibility to participate in the Tokyo Round during the 1970s.[45] Immediately before the opening of the Tokyo Round the U.S. government had determined that these trade negotiations should be open to any interested country. Ironically, the American decision to open the Tokyo Round to any interested country (a decision that was made in the era of détente) was taken specifically to invite Soviet participation in the multilateral trade negotiations.[46]

Bulgaria was not eligible to participate in the Uruguay Round under any of the criteria stated in the ministerial declaration of 1986. Bulgaria's participation under the fifth clause on developing countries was blocked because neither the United States nor the EC would recognize Bulgaria as a developing country, although others including Norway did so. The American and Community's position marked a sharp departure from conventional institutional practices. This was the first time in the history of the GATT that a country was not granted developing status on the basis of self-selection.[47]

Bulgaria's participation under the fourth clause, which allowed for Chinese participation, was also blocked. The Bulgarian government had indeed notified the contracting parties of its intention to negotiate the terms of its membership as a contracting party before the ministerial declaration of September 25. But this application had not yet been submitted to a regular meeting of the Council of Representatives—the stated rule for eligibility to participate in the Uruguay Round.

Bulgaria's Bid

Despite being denied the opportunity to participate in the Uruguay Round, Bulgarian officials continued to make substantial efforts to obtain approval for some parts of the application that they had submitted in September 1986. They did not press the issues that had received a firmly negative response any further; the attempts to participate in the Uruguay Round and to be recognized as a developing country were abandoned. However, Bulgarian officials had many informal meetings with representatives of the major contracting parties and members of the secretariat during the fall of 1986 to discuss the subject of accession per se. The main focus of the discussions centered on establishing a working party to consider Bulgaria's accession to the GATT through the regular provision of article 33 of the General Agreement. These informal meetings generated some positive results. When the Bulgarian application of September 8 was presented to a council meeting in October, only the United States opposed establishing a working party on Bulgaria. U.S. opposition, however, was enough to temporarily block the application.

Establishing a Working Party

The united transatlantic opposition to Bulgaria's participation in the Uruguay Round had disintegrated. The United States firmly opposed agreeing to any Bulgarian requests, while the Community wanted to separate the issue of participation in the Uruguay Round and the issue of establishing a working party to consider accession.[48] The EC opposed Bulgaria's participation in the Uruguay Round but was less resistant to setting up a working party.

The different positions adopted by the United States and the EC in the fall of 1986 were somewhat out of character with past negotiations. The EC had previously been particularly hostile to Bulgaria. Furthermore, the discussions over whether an Eastern European country should be allowed to accede to the GATT had generally elicited a united transatlantic response. Discussions over the terms of agreement, on the other hand, had traditionally caused transatlantic disputes. To understand why a new pattern began to emerge, one has to look at the broader changes that were taking place in the Community's bilateral relations with the East. The EC's more forthcoming approach in the GATT forum was adopted in the context of the broader thaw in EC-Eastern European relations that was occurring at that time. Negotiations over the EC-CMEA Joint Declaration were progressing, and improved relations between the two halves of Europe led the Community to be less antagonistic toward matters in the GATT forum.[49] Furthermore, Community officials believed it would not be difficult to stall negotiations between Bulgaria and the

GATT even if a working party was established. They apparently thought it would be easy to use delaying tactics, such as finding problems in selecting an appropriate chair, should circumstances call for them.[50]

The Bulgarian request to establish a working party to consider its accession to the GATT was raised again at the next council meeting on November 5 and 6. This time the United States approved the application because it was uneasy at being totally isolated at the prior meeting.[51] The EC's more forthcoming approach had forced the United States into line.

At this meeting in November, the council approved the establishment of a working party to consider Bulgaria's accession to the GATT. But certain issues were also mentioned that were likely to delay progress on the matter. The council specified that the working party would not meet, and a chair or terms of reference for the working party would not be decided upon until Bulgaria submitted a satisfactory memorandum on its economic system and foreign trade regime.[52]

The Bulgarian government originally intended to submit such a memorandum in the spring of 1987, after the introduction of economic reforms scheduled to be adopted at the beginning of 1987. However, submission of the memorandum was delayed until June 1988.[53] In the intervening period Bulgarian officials said they considered the Hungarian protocol of accession to be an appropriate precedent. They used arguments similar to those put forward in the Hungarian accession negotiations and explained that there was insufficient government intervention in the Bulgarian economy to undertake a quantitative import commitment. Instead, tariff concessions should be regarded as an appropriate entrance fee.[54] Bulgarian officials, like Hungarian officials in the early 1970s, also stressed that an agreement on the basis of tariff concessions would facilitate further reform of the economic system because it would enhance the power of reform-oriented policymakers in domestic policy conflicts.[55]

The Bulgarian foreign trade memorandum was submitted on June 13, 1988, along with a request that the issue be discussed at a council meeting to be held two days later. It seems, however, that the major contracting parties considered that there had been no time to study the matter. The Bulgarian delegation then asked the secretariat to begin consultations to decide the terms of reference and choose the chair for the working party, as agreed upon at the council meeting in November 1986.

Terms of Reference

The question of terms of reference for the working party generated substantial difficulties with the United States. The U.S. government strongly opposed using the standard terms of reference that were employed in other working parties that dealt with accessions. Standard terms of reference were "to examine the application of the Government of . . . to accede to the General Agreement under article XXXIII, and to submit to the Council recommendations which might include a draft protocol of accession."[56]

The U.S. government instead proposed that nonstandard terms of reference be used in the Bulgarian case, even though standard terms of reference had been used for the accession negotiations with Poland, Rumania, and Hungary. The American proposals for Bulgaria's terms of reference included a very long (and, in the opinion of many other Western officials, excessively harsh) list of issues that were to be examined in the working party. The American determination to use nonstandard terms was sufficiently pronounced to lead American representatives to approach officials from other contracting parties at the ambassadorial level in Geneva, in an attempt to obtain support. At one point the U.S. government even asked American embassies to seek support in the capitals of major contracting parties. Other governments were asked to support the approach chosen by the United States and, if the American position suited their views, to make their support clear in the relevant meetings in Geneva.[57] These requests for support, however, yielded few results.

The detailed American proposals for nonstandard terms of reference were strongly opposed by the Bulgarian government. The subject was discussed at several council meetings during the next eighteen months and at the informal meetings that were held before the relevant council meetings. The American representative apparently bluntly stated at these informal meetings that the U.S. text was the only basis on which the United States could discuss the matter.

The Community's representative, in contrast, adopted a very passive and low-key approach in these meetings and appears to have said very little. The EC voiced no objection to the American proposals during the informal meetings and was in no particular hurry to see progress on the matter in 1988 and 1989. During those years the Community apparently found it convenient to hide behind the United States. The situation was similar to the cat-and-mouse game between the United States and the EC in the earlier discussions over Bulgaria's application to accede to the standards code. But it was the United States that was left to play the leading role in the Bulgarian case in 1988 and 1989. The Community's position became slightly more forthcoming at the beginning of 1990, because of signs of change in Bulgarian politics at that time and in light of the progress in the EC's negotiations for bilateral trade agreements with individual Eastern European countries. By early 1990 the EC—like the Canadian government—was apparently not too concerned by the specific terms of reference. It considered standard terms of reference acceptable and was also willing to accept some amendments to the standard terms. But it thought that the American proposals were excessively harsh and went too far.[58]

This disagreement over the terms of reference points again to a need to go beyond the systemic economic differences noted in the official discussions, in order to understand the Western policies toward negotiations between Eastern European countries and the GATT. Although certain American officials consistently maintained that the systemic economic differences accounted for and justified the proposal for nonstandard terms of reference, other officials (including some from the United States) expressed more doubt. The American proposal for nonstandard terms of reference was perhaps best explained by one Western official, who described it as "a not very ingenious way of trying to prolong as much as possible."[59]

Systemic economic differences alone fail to explain why the United States proposed that the criteria used to evaluate the Bulgarian application should be different from those that had been used to evaluate applications from other nonmarket-economy countries such as Rumania. A possibly more convincing explanation for the U.S. position toward the terms of reference was that broader political-strategic issues were not conducive to cooperation with Bulgaria. A focus on political rather than trade policy issues would also help to explain why the United States was to subsequently back down and concede to a compromise agreement in early 1990.

The Post-Cold-War World

The dispute on terms of reference was finally resolved in February 1990. Agreement was reached on a compromise text that had apparently been proposed but deemed unacceptable more than one year earlier, in January 1989. The final agreement included the standard terms of reference with one additional sentence stating, "It is understood that in its examination, the Working Party will consider the compatibility of Bulgaria's foreign trade regime with the General Agreement with regard, inter alia, to the provisions concerning national treatment, non-discrimination, State-trading, subsidies and safeguards."[60] The United States agreed to substantially shorten and soften the lengthy and harsh terms initially proposed. Bulgaria, on its part, agreed to this one additional sentence.

The American government's desire to have nonstandard terms of reference was accommodated insofar as the additional sentence cited above was agreed upon. However, the U.S. willingness to modify its initial proposal (which had apparently previously been declared the only basis on which the United States could discuss the matter) did signify an important change in attitude. Agreement to more reasonable terms by the United States opened the path for a meeting of the working party.

The political changes taking place in Bulgaria at that time had led to a shift in the overall American approach toward Bulgaria. This was evident when Secretary of State James Baker visited Bulgaria in February 1990. Baker was the most senior U.S. official to visit the country since World War II. This larger political context apparently affected the negotiations in the GATT forum and contributed to the slightly more open-minded approach taken by the United States in February 1990. In addition, the change in the American position resulted from its growing isolation in the GATT forum.[61]

Little concrete progress was made on the Bulgarian application during the course of the next year, owing to delaying tactics on all sides—a result of the uncertain situation in Bulgaria and the changes in Bulgarian economic legislation. In accordance with conventional institutional practice, contracting parties were invited to pose written questions on the foreign trade memorandum. Although some contracting parties submitted questions by the scheduled deadline of the summer of 1990, both the EC and the United States apparently delayed posing their questions until December 1990 and February 1991, respectively. The Bulgarian government itself then delayed responding for several months. The responses that arrived in June 1991 were unusually brief compared with the normal practice in the GATT forum. Often they simply stated that the question was no longer applicable because of changes being made in Bulgarian domestic legislation.[62]

The Future

How the negotiations between Bulgaria and the GATT proceed in the future will obviously partly depend on the Bulgarian side. Meaningful reform of the economy would remove the trade policy dilemmas posed by a nonmarket country. However, a real and thorough transformation of the economic system will take some time, and the task of addressing Bulgaria's application remains.

The more important issues at stake in Bulgaria's bid to join the GATT have stemmed from the lack of Western political will to cooperate with Bulgaria (particularly during the new cold war of the early 1980s), the fact that the Bulgarian case became enmeshed in the Soviet case, and—for the Community—the desire to first resolve problems in bilateral relations with the East. This indicates that the future negotiations with Bulgaria will in part depend on issues that have little to do with economic reform in that country; namely, on the extent to which Western governments restructure their policies in light of fundamental changes that are occurring in the more important issues.

The new environment of the post-cold-war world has removed the strategic rationale for treating Bulgaria less favorably than other Eastern countries. Western positions are beginning to adjust, and Western governments are beginning to adopt a more open-minded position. But there is still a long way to go. It may take some time before Bulgaria becomes disentangled from the former Soviet Union in the eyes of some Western officials, and the fear of creating a precedent for such larger nonmarket countries as Russia (and China) is likely to have some impact on the negotiations over the terms of agreement. Future negotiations over trade policy issues may therefore be tough. Some progress has been made, however, and Bulgaria's accession to the GATT is now on the agenda. Changes in the broader political issues at stake leave the West little alternative but to permit Bulgaria to join the international trade institution. As one Western European official interviewed in 1990 stated, "It would be inconsistent with our broader policy towards the East to exclude Bulgaria from the GATT."[63]

Chapter 6

The Primacy of Politics: The Soviet Union and the GATT

THE STATED REASON for opposing Soviet bids for affiliation with the GATT in the 1980s centered on the trade policy dilemmas raised by systemic economic differences. However, the international economic organizations created at the end of World War II were originally expected to have a broad membership. The Soviet Union—as a wartime ally of the United States and Great Britain, the two principal countries responsible for designing the postwar international economic order—was strongly encouraged to participate in the envisioned institutions. The different nature of the Soviet economic system was not seen as an obstacle to integration. Instead, the postwar planners considered various provisions that might accommodate a nonmarket country.

The Suggested Charter for an International Trade Organization, put forward for discussion by the United States in 1946, included two articles that would have facilitated Soviet participation. Article 28 included a variant of the quantitative import commitment inserted into many bilateral agreements with the Soviet Union in the interwar years. The clause specified that a country with a complete or substantially complete monopoly of its import trade should undertake a global import commitment, of an amount to be agreed upon, in reciprocation of the tariff concessions granted by market countries. A commercial considerations clause, designed to ensure that the increased trade arising from the import commitment be conducted in a nondiscriminatory manner, was simultaneously inserted in the Suggested Charter as article 26.[1]

Soviet participation in the IMF and the World Bank was likewise encouraged. A draft of the White Plan for the International Monetary Fund, written in 1942, included a note stating:

No restrictions as to membership should be imposed on grounds of the particular economic structure adopted by any country. . . .

To exclude a country such as Russia would be an egregious error. Russia, despite her socialist economy, could both contribute and profit by participation. To deny her the privileges of joining in this cooperative effort to improve world economic relations would be to repeat the tragic errors of the last generation, and introduce a very discordant note.[2]

The Soviet Union was an active participant in the preparation of the charters for the IMF and the World Bank. Exploratory discussions with Soviet representatives were held as early as 1943. American and Soviet officials then engaged in informal negotiations on the subject in early 1944. The USSR participated in the Bretton Woods Conference in July 1944, where the articles of agreement for the fund and the bank were finalized, and the Soviet government signed the agreement emerging from the conference.[3]

The political atmosphere between the wartime allies then deteriorated rapidly. The USSR abstained from joining the two financial institutions and failed to attend the conferences where the draft charter for the ITO was discussed. Cold war politics filtered through into the Soviet position toward economic relations with the West in a manner similar to the American approach toward economic relations with the East. The Soviet government adopted a hostile approach toward institutions such as the GATT and the IMF during the height of the cold war era in the 1950s.

Initial Approaches, 1980s

Soviet hostility toward the GATT at the height of the cold war became muted by the 1960s. Ever since there have been indirect, informal contacts between middle-level officials from the Soviet mission in Geneva and a few members of the GATT secretariat at social functions and in the corridors of formal meetings such as the Economic Commission for Europe (ECE) discussions. More direct Soviet approaches began in a tentative manner at the end of 1979. But it was only in the early 1980s that the USSR expressed some serious interest in possible affiliation with the institution and developed more formal contacts with the GATT.[4]

Soviet officials began to approach some contracting parties at the beginning of 1983 to ask what might happen should the USSR ask for observer status. Observer status at sessions of the contracting parties and at the council meetings usually entitles a government to attend all meetings except those of the budget committee, to speak at these meetings after full members have spoken, and to receive copies of GATT documents. Observer status provides no voting rights.[5]

The Soviet government also informed the secretariat that it was having these conversations with some contracting parties, and the Soviet ambassador in Geneva apparently held a meeting with the director-general of the GATT, Arthur Dunkel. Similar approaches to some contracting parties were made the following year, and Soviet officials again informed the secretariat about the contacts.

The Soviet approaches elicited a firmly negative response from the United States and the Community. However, the General Agreement included no criteria for obtaining observer status, leaving the United States and the EC with little official justification for opposing a Soviet request. Western officials nevertheless managed to employ various strategies that blocked any possible chance for the Soviet Union to succeed in its bid to become an observer.

American and Western European officials initially opposed the Soviet request on the basis of rules they had merely proposed for adoption. Western officials were at that time considering rules to determine a country's eligibility to become an observer, and they initiated informal consultations on the matter in the GATT. One proposed rule was that a country applying for observer status should express interest in subsequently increasing its ties with the GATT. Because the USSR at that time had not expressed such an interest, Western officials cited the proposed rule and informed the USSR that it would not be eligible for observer status.[6]

The Western strategy changed in 1986, when it became evident that it would be difficult to devise new rules that would effectively bar only one or two specific countries from observer status. Moreover, Western officials realized that the USSR or other applicants could circumvent such rules. For example, it would be easy for the Soviet Union to say it was interested in further affiliation with the GATT. American and Western European officials therefore abandoned attempts to draw up specific rules. Instead they decided to delay completion of the review on criteria for obtaining observer status and to announce that they would approve no new applications until completion of the review, an outcome they could delay indefinitely. The informal consultations on rules and procedures were put aside, and American and Community representatives informed a meeting of the council that no further requests for observer status would be granted until the review was concluded.[7] This position was clearly stated in an internal American document written in the early fall of 1986:

> At the last GATT Council meeting, the EC and the United States indicated that, pending the completion of a review of the issue of criteria for observership, neither would consider the approval of applicants. . . .
>
> Since GATT observership is granted on the basis of consensus, and since neither the U.S. nor the EC will agree to additional observerships, pending the completion of the CPS review, a Soviet request for observership at this time could not be considered.[8]

The Soviet Union subsequently changed its focus to an attempt to participate in the Uruguay Round, a desire that was first officially announced in December 1985 at a UN,ECE meeting.[9] Several months later, in August 1986, the Soviet government officially notified the GATT of its desire to participate in the Uruguay Round that was to be launched at Punta del Este in September 1986. This application was barred by very strict new rules announced in the ministerial declaration of September 25, 1986, that were written specifically to block Soviet and Bulgarian participation in the Uruguay Round.[10] The Soviet application was essentially ignored at the meeting in Punta del Este.[11] There was no formal discussion on the subject.[12]

Western Positions

The Western countries adopted a united, negative position toward the Soviet Union in the 1980s that differed sharply from the encouraging approach taken by the postwar planners. The reasons for opposing the Soviet approaches during the 1980s shed light on the constraints against and opportunities for participation by the Soviet Union's successor states in the future. The reasons were complex, making it difficult to disentangle rhetoric from reality. While public statements by government officials focused almost exclusively on trade policy issues, it is clear that other issues were involved. All the issues dictated opposition to the Soviet requests.

Strategic considerations provide a good starting point. There has always been a strong correlation between the West's security policy toward the USSR and the West's position toward Soviet participation in the GATT. Before the outbreak of the cold war the USSR was invited to participate in the negotiations over a charter for the proposed ITO. During the era of détente, the United States advocated opening the Tokyo Round to any interested country, a strategy again designed to encourage Soviet participation.[13] In the early and mid-1980s, however, the Western position was reversed, as is evident from the fact that officials were devising criteria for the Uruguay Round that would specifically bar the Soviet Union. And in late 1989, with the changes in the geostrategic environment and the move beyond containment, there was yet another reversal in the West's attitude toward Soviet affiliation, as discussed below. A focus on the systemic economic differences noted in official statements fails to explain this pattern, because the nature of the Soviet economic system was essentially constant throughout this period. Once again, the broader political climate and East-West security relations set the context.

The West's responses to Soviet applications in the 1980s were also influenced by trade policy and institutional considerations. The potential size of Soviet trading capabilities have made economic policy issues a greater concern than in the negotiations with smaller Eastern European countries. The systemic economic differences were relevant during the negotiations on accepting Soviet applications to participate in the GATT. Some Western officials, particularly those who were more directly immersed in GATT affairs, feared that participation by a major nonmarket country could contribute to a dilution or erosion of the market-oriented rules of the GATT.

Finally, many officials in both the United States and Western Europe feared that Soviet participation might lead to an "UNCTAD-ization" of the GATT. They worried that the USSR might alter the GATT's pragmatic approach, politicizing the institution by turning it into a forum similar to the United Nations Conference on Trade and Development for raising broader East-West and North-South disputes. This would not only disrupt the businesslike approach taken in the GATT but would also reduce the favored Eastern European countries' freedom for maneuver.

In short, several issues led the West to block Soviet participation in the 1980s: the political and security climate, the dilution of market-oriented GATT rules, and the UNCTAD-ization of GATT.[14] The relative importance of these factors was apparent in the following statement by an official interviewed in 1988:

> The fear is that the Soviet Union will lead to a politicization of the GATT. It could undermine the rules as well and lead to increasingly different interpretations of the rules. But this isn't really an issue. There's already many deviations from MFN, like customs unions. The East European issue is just another one of many. One can question the value of the MFN principle. The GATT is very adaptable. Deviation from MFN doesn't necessarily mean GATT would collapse. Fear of undermining MFN would factor into the decision if there were political changes leading to encouraging the Soviet Union—but we'd look for a way of living with it if the political climate was favorable enough, as with China. Things would move to the OECD.[15]

The End of the Cold War

The Malta summit in December 1989 was hailed by many as symbolizing the end of the cold war. Among other matters, President Bush announced that the United States would support a Soviet application to become an observer at the GATT after the conclusion of the Uruguay Round. Several days later, at the EC summit in Strasbourg, the EC announced support for granting the Soviet Union observer status. The change in the political-security climate had removed a major constraint against Soviet affiliation with the GATT.

The Soviet Union officially applied for observer status in early March 1990.[16] Director-General Dunkel became actively involved and held informal consultations with approximately thirty contracting parties.[17] These meetings revealed that only two contracting parties, the United States and Japan, had reservations. All others believed that the Soviet application should be immediately approved.[18]

The United States initially favored granting the Soviet Union observer status only after the conclusion of the Uruguay Round. Apparently no other contracting party could fully comprehend the rationale behind the American position. It seems that the initial decision to grant observer status after the Uruguay Round had largely emerged from intragovernmental conflicts. The position had apparently been adopted as a "compromise statement" that owed at least as much to interdepartmental politics as to international politics.[19] Possible Soviet observer status had generated a fair degree of conflict within the United States government for several months before the Malta summit. Some parts of the government, particularly officials in the Office of the United States Trade Representative (USTR), had strongly opposed granting observer status for fear that this would undermine the integrity of the international trade institution. Others, particularly officials in the State Department working on bilateral relations with the Soviet Union, had favored granting observer status as a positive symbolic gesture to the USSR.[20] Granting observer status after the conclusion of the Uruguay Round split the difference.

The United States changed its position relatively quickly in the spring of 1990, when the consensus in the GATT forced the U.S. government to rethink the matter. It seems that more careful thought led to the conclusion that there was little logical reason for delaying approval of the Soviet application.[21]

Political issues concerning security apparently contributed to the Japanese government's reservations. Officials responsible for bilateral relations with the Soviet Union were actively involved in the decisionmaking process on this GATT issue and viewed the subject as a political matter. Japanese-Soviet relations had not yet entered the post-cold-war era, and the unresolved territorial dispute over the Kurile Islands apparently contributed to the Japanese government's less forthcoming approach toward Soviet affiliation with the GATT.[22]

The Community adopted a significantly more forthcoming approach than either the United States or Japan, contributing to differences within the Western alliance similar to those that had occurred in the negotiations with Bulgaria in the late 1980s. It seems that this more positive position was partly attributable to the broader changes in the EC's bilateral relations with the East, signaled by the conclusion of the EC-CMEA Joint Declaration in 1988. The USSR had clearly abandoned its prior position of hostility toward the Community and concluded a bilateral trade and cooperation agreement with the EC in December 1989. This new Soviet approach generated a forthcoming response from the Community and a sense that the USSR "should be paid back."[23]

The Soviet application for observer status was the first item on the agenda at the council meeting in May 1990. A positive decision was taken, the request was approved, and no overt friction occurred. All contracting parties approved the request, and representatives of many contracting parties said they "warmly welcomed" the USSR as an observer. However, both the American and Japanese representatives, while "welcoming" the USSR, firmly stressed that observer status was a very different issue from full membership and that the decision on observer status should in no way prejudge a possible future application for accession to full membership. This point was omitted (perhaps diplomatically) from the speech made by the representative of the Community.[24]

Attaining observer status at the GATT was an important symbolic step toward integration into the global economy. Whether this position will be maintained by the Soviet Union's successor states in the next few years remains an open question. Western governments had pressed for what amounted to an escape clause in order to give themselves the ability to alter the agreement should events require a change. The United States, Japan, and the Community had apparently all insisted that the rights and obligations of observers be reviewed at the end of 1992 and that any rules emerging from the review would be applied to the USSR. Hence Soviet observer status was effectively guaranteed only until the end of 1992. Until that time it was understood that conventional practices relating to observers be applied to the Soviet Union.[25] The issue now concerns granting observer status to the Soviet Union's successor states beyond 1992, and decisions need to be taken.

Chapter 7

The Soviet Union's Successor States and the Global Economy

THE LEADERS of the world's seven main industrialized countries, gathering in July 1991 for the annual Group of Seven (G-7) summit, reached an agreement "to assist the integration of the Soviet Union into the world economy."[1] Mikhail Gorbachev, president of the Soviet Union, was invited to meet with the G-7 leaders at the end of the summit—a meeting that Britain's Prime Minister John Major described as a day "that history may well see as a landmark. It will be seen as a first step toward helping the Soviet Union become a full member of the world economic community."[2] The discussions considered the problems of the Soviet economy and appropriate forms of Western assistance. They resulted in the G-7's agreement to grant the Soviet Union greater technical aid and associate agreements with the IMF and the World Bank.

Several weeks later the West was extremely disturbed at the news that Gorbachev had been removed from power in a coup led by Soviet hard-liners. The agreements reached at the G-7 summit were placed on hold as the immediate crisis unfolded on August 19, 1991. The hard-liners' attempts to regain power proved to be a failure. The episode instead served to demonstrate the incredible changes that had taken place in the Soviet Union since Gorbachev rose to power in 1985. The enormity of the changes was further clarified in December 1991, when the Soviet Union was dissolved and replaced by the new sovereign states of Armenia, Azerbaijan, Belorussia, Georgia, Kazakhstan, Kirghizia, Moldavia, Russia, Tajikistan, Turkmenistan, Ukraine, and Uzbekistan. The situation in some of the Soviet Union's successor states is still uncertain, and it remains to be seen what will emerge in the next decade from the clashes between the forces urging change and those defending the status quo. Meanwhile the West is left with no choice but to adapt quickly to the new realities and develop appropriate policies toward the new sovereign states in the face of this uncertainty.

The purpose of this concluding chapter is to contribute to that task by focusing on the new states' affiliation with the GATT. The conclusions that can be learned from past cases regarding Soviet and Eastern European negotiations with the GATT are first reviewed. Drawing on these lessons from the past, the discussion then turns to the pros and cons of alternative policies that may be adopted toward relations between the Soviet Union's successor states and the GATT in the future.

The Soviet Union, Eastern Europe, and the GATT: A Summary

The issues at stake in the negotiations between the Soviet Union, Eastern Europe, and the GATT varied according to the stage of negotiation. Political-security issues set the context and determined the criteria for agreement. In subsequent stages trade policy issues emerged, influencing the negotiations over the terms and implementation of agreements.

The Primacy of Politics

The first conclusion that can be drawn is that political issues are the main driving force behind negotiations regarding Eastern participation in the GATT. The outcomes of the negotiations have been primarily determined by Western political objectives in the East, and good relations with the West have been a necessary precondition for ensuring that an application is placed on the agenda and given serious consideration. This conclusion holds for the cases examined in both the cold war and the post-cold-war world.

The policy of differentiation, whose strategic goal was to reduce Soviet influence in Eastern Europe, dictated Western cooperation with Poland, Rumania, and Hungary, and conflict with Bulgaria. The West accordingly supported the three favored nonmarket countries in their bids to join the GATT and blocked the applications submitted by Bulgaria, a country viewed by many Western officials as a close Soviet ally during the cold war.

Similar lessons can be learned from the negotiations in the post-cold-war world. Broader political changes in the East since the late 1980s have begun to filter through into the negotiations in the GATT forum, and the process of restructuring Western policies has been started. The EC adopted a less hostile position toward Bulgaria as relations between the two halves of Europe began to normalize through the negotiation of the EC-CMEA Joint Declaration and the conclusion of bilateral trade agreements between the EC and Eastern European countries. These broader changes were intensified as a result of the dramatic political events in Eastern Europe in 1989. The EC accordingly adopted a somewhat more positive posture toward Bulgaria and shifted its position on the long-standing dispute on discriminatory quantitative restrictions with Hungary and Poland, even though these countries had barely started to reform their economic systems. Similarly, the United States adopted a somewhat more open-minded approach toward Bulgaria in the spring of 1990 and agreed to a compromise settlement on the terms of reference for the working party established to deal with Bulgaria's application to join the GATT.

Similar lessons can also be learned from the Soviet case. Western positions toward Soviet affiliation with the international trade institution have varied over time in accordance with shifts in broader political-security policies. Western positions ranged from the decision to open the Tokyo Round negotiations to any interested country so as to invite Soviet participation during the détente era of the 1970s, to the denial of observer status during the new cold war of the 1980s, and finally to the decision to grant observer status during the post-cold-war world.

Conflicts within the West were rare during the stage of the negotiations concerned with the question of whether to accept an application. Western countries were united when political-security issues were at stake, although some differences began to emerge in the late 1980s, when the Community adopted a more open-minded position toward matters in the GATT forum after the resolution of its particular problems in bilateral relations with the East. Given the normalization of the EC's relations with the East since the late 1980s, one may expect that the EC's position toward negotiations with the East in the GATT forum will remain more forthcoming than that of either the United States or Japan.

Other possible factors that may have influenced Western decisionmaking fail to provide a consistent explanation for the outcome of negotiations regarding Soviet and Eastern European participation in the GATT. Systemic economic differences between the Eastern countries and the market-oriented principles of the GATT give little insight into the negotiations with the smaller Eastern European countries. Furthermore, although systemic economic differences have had more influence over decisionmaking in the Soviet case owing to the potentially large size of Soviet trading capabilities, they fail to provide a consistent explanation for Western policies toward the negotiations with the Soviet Union. Western policies have varied over time, yet the nature of the Soviet economic system remained essentially constant throughout the period examined.

It could be proposed that Bulgaria's and the Soviet Union's failed attempts resulted from the fact that the GATT was frailer in the 1980s than in earlier decades when Poland, Rumania, and Hungary joined. This greater frailty may have generated increasing Western opposition to applications from nonmarket countries out of fear that the need to bend GATT rules might further dilute and undermine the cohesion of the trade institution's liberal framework. Yet this possible institutional concern fails to explain why Western governments adopted a more open-minded position toward Bulgaria and the Soviet Union at the end of the 1980s and beginning of the 1990s, at a time when the future of the GATT was most uncertain, given the stalled negotiations for the Uruguay Round. The GATT was more fragile at this time than it had been in earlier negotiations with Bulgaria and the Soviet Union.[3]

Trade Policy Conflicts

The second main conclusion that can be drawn from this study is that the trade policy issues at stake in the negotiations over the terms of agreement between nonmarket countries and the GATT cause a fair degree of West-West conflict. Conflict within the West was more pronounced when trade policy issues came to the forefront and political-security issues slid into the background. The negotiations over terms and implementation of agreements often became enmeshed in broader debates over nondiscrimination. The conflicting pressures behind the negotiations often had little to do with Eastern Europe per se, but were instead typical of many other negotiations in which questions about nonmarket economic systems were absent.

Because of the emergence of broader transatlantic conflicts over nondiscrimination—a principal norm of the GATT—the negotiations generated a pattern of alignment that was rarely seen in East-West trade negotiations outside the GATT forum. The cooperation between the United States and the socialist countries in their conflict with the Community was explained by the American determination to bring economic relations into the multilateral GATT framework.

The United States, with few commercial interests at stake, championed nondiscrimination. The traditional American opposition to discriminatory QRs that prevailed in the 1940s resurfaced in these specific negotiations with the East. Likewise the broader American determination to halt a proliferation of the Community's preferential trade agreements resurfaced during the negotiations with Rumania in 1980. In contrast, the EC, with somewhat greater commercial interests at stake, often failed to uphold nondiscrimination and instead championed reciprocity. This was demonstrated by the maintenance of discriminatory QRs against the Eastern GATT members, the unwillingness to approve Hungary's request that tariff concessions be accepted as a legitimate entrance fee, and the problematical clause inserted in the bilateral agreement reached with Rumania in 1980. The opposing stances taken on the two sides of the Atlantic were also evident at the early stages of the negotiations over Bulgaria's application to join the standards code. The transatlantic differences toward the question of a discriminatory safeguard clause in the early stages of these negotiations reflected a broader U.S.-EC dispute that had taken place in the 1970s, when there had been an attempt to revise the main GATT safeguard clause.

Implications

The primacy of political issues in the negotiations between Eastern countries and the GATT leads one to expect that the subject of participation by the Soviet Union's successor states will be an important item on the agenda for the 1990s, regardless of the pace at which economic reform proceeds in those countries. This suggests that those Western trade policy officials who are sincerely concerned about the systemic economic differences will be left with little alternative but to find ways to accommodate the new states' participation in the GATT should Western political objectives dictate cooperation.

However, when trade policy issues arise as an item of discussion during the negotiations over terms of agreement, some conflict can be expected.

The Future

The subject of trade with the Soviet Union has for many years generated substantial conflict in the West, although the range of policy options under debate has varied greatly over time. For example, during the early 1980s there was intense debate on the use of the Reagan administration's policy of exclusion, designed to deny the Soviet Union the benefits of trade. In the late 1980s the debate shifted to positive engagement, culminating in a rare degree of Western consensus at the beginning of the 1990s in favor of a policy of inclusion, which stressed the need to integrate the Soviet Union into the global economy. This positive posture was reaffirmed in January 1992, after the collapse of the Soviet Union, when the West embarked on negotiations to integrate such successor states as Russia, Ukraine, and Kazakhstan into the IMF and the World Bank. But even this consensus masks differences that will emerge in discussions over specific details.

The future of Western debates on trade with the sovereign states of the former Soviet Union obviously depends partly on how political and economic events in those countries develop. Reformers currently have the upper hand in countries like Kazakhstan, Russia, and Ukraine. But the situation is fragile and setbacks may recur. Although the leaders of these new states are committed to integration into the global economy, it is not clear how much freedom they will have to implement policies designed to speed economic reform. Some people in these countries still oppose change. Compromise with the defenders of the status quo may be required, particularly if unemployment and food shortages increase. Transformation of the economy will not occur overnight. Nonetheless, the forces of change are now profound and powerful and do not hinge on a single leader. Western countries therefore have to fully restructure their policies toward economic relations with the former Soviet Union and face the task of helping to integrate reforming nonmarket countries into the global economy.

I now turn to one area in which the West will have to think through its position in the future—relations between the Soviet Union's successor states and the GATT—and discuss the implications of several different policy options. This topic highlights some of the conflicting pressures that will also emerge in discussions on other aspects of Western economic policies toward the new sovereign states.

Observer Status

As noted in chapter 6, the Soviet Union was effectively guaranteed observer status at the GATT only until the end of 1992. It was agreed that the rights and obligations for observer status would be reviewed then and that any new rules which emerged would apply to the Soviet Union. This agreement provided an escape clause that would have enabled the West to halt the Soviet Union's status as an observer if political events had developed in a manner that dictated returning to a policy of exclusion. The subsequent collapse of the Soviet Union requires the Western countries to consider immediately whether they will allow the successor states to be observers at the GATT beyond the end of 1992.

It is generally accepted that the West should pursue a policy of inclusion toward the new sovereign states, and this policy clearly requires granting continued observer status at the GATT. Observer status is more symbolic than substantive and presents no technical economic dilemmas. While it provides an opportunity for officials from the new sovereign states to become acquainted with the norms and rules of the institution, it grants none of the benefits of GATT membership. Some Western trade policy officials, particularly those in the Office of the United States Trade Representative, may oppose granting observer status to the new countries until they adopt an economic system compatible with the market-oriented rules of the international trading system, in the same way as they opposed granting the Soviet Union observer status in early 1990. However, history indicates that trade policy considerations will not have a substantial impact on the final decisions adopted by Western governments. This was evident during the discussions over the Soviet Union's application for observer status in the spring of 1990. At that time opposition by American trade policy officials was overwhelmed when others in the U.S. government, after being forced by the consensus in the GATT forum to think through the issue carefully, concluded that there was little reason to delay approval of the Soviet application. One can therefore expect that the Western countries will open the path to continued observer states for those new sovereign states toward which they extend the policy of inclusion.

Associate Agreement

The discussions at the G-7 summit in July 1991 focused on Soviet affiliation with the IMF and the World Bank, and concluded with a decision to grant the Soviet Union an associate agreement with these two institutions. After the collapse of the Soviet Union in December 1991, the West speedily adapted to the new political situation, announcing that such countries as Kazakhstan, Russia, and Ukraine could become full members of the IMF and the World Bank even though they still had a long way to go before completing the transformation to a market economy. It has not yet been announced that a similar policy will be adopted toward these countries' affiliation with the GATT.

Full membership in the GATT will clearly require paying attention to trade policy problems raised by a nonmarket country's participation. However, an intermediary step could have been taken at the G-7 summit and could be relatively easily adopted in the immediate future without lengthy technical economic discussions: to grant the Soviet Union's successor states associate agreements with the GATT.

Precedents exist. As noted in chapter 3, Poland was granted an associate agreement in 1959, at a time when the West was not yet ready to approve Poland's request to accede to full membership. The desire to give Poland some encouragement led to this compromise. It stated that the signatories, being guided by the objectives set out in the Preamble to the General Agreement on Tariffs and Trade, desired to expand their trade on the basis of mutual advantage in trading conditions and opportunities. The agreement obliged the signatories to give sympathetic consideration to any concerns relating to the implementation of this commitment and provided for annual reviews to oversee the implementation stage.

Associate agreements had also previously been reached with Japan and Yugoslavia in 1953 and 1959, respectively. The agreement reached with Yugoslavia involved somewhat more substantive commitments than the Polish agreement. For example, although both agreements provided for annual consultations to oversee the implementation stage, only the Yugoslav agreement stated that the annual meetings would review the possibilities of further progress toward the full application of the General Agreement. Finally, the agreements included escape clauses that would easily allow a signatory to withdraw from the agreement.[4]

Granting the Soviet Union's successor states associate agreements with the GATT in the immediate future poses little risk to anyone as a transitional measure. Some Western trade policy officials would no doubt lack enthusiasm for such agreements, in the same way they opposed granting the Soviet Union observer status. They might argue that associate agreements would open the path to accession to full membership in the international trade institution—an outcome that in their view should be avoided until the applicants adopt an economic system compatible with the market-oriented rules of the GATT. However, the possibility of serious consideration of these countries' accession to full membership is on the agenda for the post-cold-war world as long as reformers remain in power in the new sovereign states.

The political issues that favor granting reformist countries like Russia an associate agreement with the GATT appear to be evident. In brief, the strategic landscape of the post-cold-war world provides no rationale for excluding these countries from the economic institutions of the global community. The new sovereign states pose little direct military threat to the West now that the former Soviet Union's troops are largely out of Eastern Europe. To the contrary, political-security considerations mandate adopting a policy of inclusion toward such countries as Kazakhstan and Russia in order to maintain a cooperative atmosphere conducive to the implementation of arms reduction agreements, the withdrawal of remaining troops from eastern Germany, and conflict resolution in areas like the Middle East.

Events in some of the Soviet Union's successor states could change, and hard-liners could regain power. Under these conditions the arguments in favor of allowing such states to maintain associate agreements with the GATT could become more questionable. However, the associate agreements could follow precedent and include an escape clause that would provide an exit for those GATT members that wanted to withdraw from the agreement.

Of course it remains to be seen whether the governments of countries like Russia and Ukraine would want associate agreements. Reformers in these countries might prefer to move directly to the stage of negotiations for full accession. But accession negotiations pose more complex trade policy issues and will take some time. An associate agreement could be negotiated quickly and could perhaps be made appealing to reformers in the former Soviet Union if it included a clause, similar to the one inserted in the Yugoslav agreement, which noted that the consultations would review the possibilities of further progress toward the full application of the General Agreement.

Accession to Membership

Many conflicting pressures emerge when one considers the new states' accession to full membership in the GATT, rendering the subject more complex than that of observer status or associate agreements. Political-security issues and certain trade policy issues dictate adopting a favorable approach, whereas other trade policy issues necessitate caution.

Political Issues

Should the new sovereign states such as Russia continue to adopt the cooperative foreign policy toward the West that was initiated by the Soviet Union under Gorbachev's leadership, then it seems inevitable that these countries will become members of the GATT within a reasonable period of time. This is likely to occur even if it requires admitting reforming nonmarket countries into the international trade institution.

Western leaders have announced their desire to welcome such countries as Kazakhstan and Ukraine into the global community. A logical extension of this policy is to open the path to participation in the major international trade institution. It is unreasonable and undiplomatic to expect cooperation in other areas of world politics if these countries are denied entry into the principal institutions of the global community.

Participation in international economic institutions may also have a small influence on the politics of economic reform within the new independent states and may help to move their domestic policies in a direction compatible with the interests of many other countries. International commitments undertaken by these states upon accession to the GATT could enhance the bargaining power of reform-oriented policymakers in domestic policy conflicts, at least at the margin.[5] Apart from anything else, affiliation with the GATT would expose more officials from the reforming nonmarket countries to the principles on which market economic systems are based. Accession negotiations alone would probably last for several years and could serve as a learning experience. As one Hungarian official interviewed in 1986 stated, "GATT changes people's whole outlook and minds. . . . Without GATT membership we wouldn't even know about anti-dumping."[6]

Trade Policy Issues

The implications of the new states' participation in the GATT do not, however, stop at this point. Some important trade policy issues complicate the picture and pose substantial dilemmas. The systemic economic differences pointed to by government officials in public statements regarding the Soviet Union in the 1980s also present problems. Before reviewing these it is appropriate to discuss a trade policy issue that dictates a positive approach. It was omitted from official statements in the 1980s, which discussed only negative factors.

One important trade policy consideration is maintaining an integrated global economy and avoiding a disintegration into regionalism or bilateralism. This concern lends support to a positive or open-minded approach toward participation in the GATT by the new independent states; it motivated the postwar planners to adopt a universal approach and consider ways to accommodate Soviet participation in international economic organizations. A similar approach was taken by the United States in the 1960s and 1970s. Once the United States had taken the political decision to trade with an Eastern European country, it strongly favored that country's inclusion in the multilateral GATT framework and pushed for terms of agreement that would promote nondiscrimination. Indeed, American support for multilateralism was sufficient to generate a somewhat strange pattern of West-West conflict over these East-West trade negotiations.

To uphold multilateralism today likewise requires accommodating the new states' participation in the GATT. The GATT provides a forum for preventing a proliferation of bilateral and discriminatory trade practices with these new countries. As was often noted by

Western trade policy officials who opposed Soviet participation in the GATT, the USSR was a country with potentially major trading capabilities, and the Soviet Union could have had a significant effect on the global trading system. The same is true for Russia as an individual nation, or the successor states as a group. As was far less often noted by such officials, failure to accommodate the former Soviet Union's participation in the GATT leaves bilateralism as the alternative. Exclusion may therefore have undesirable long-run implications. Encouraging trade through bilateral routes with countries that have potentially major trading capabilities may contribute to an erosion of the multilateral orientation of the postwar economic order. This aspect of the international trading system was already fragile by mid-1991, and there are many signs of a trend away from multilateralism. According to a GATT secretariat report written in 1991, "The European Community maintains a multi-layer system of trade preferences vis-à-vis third countries on a reciprocal or unilateral basis."[7] The United States now appears to be setting out on a similar path. Having concluded a bilateral trade agreement with Canada, it is now conducting negotiations for a bilateral trade agreement with Mexico. As Richard Feinberg noted in 1989, to the degree that the Soviet economy affects the global trading system, an institution that seeks to provide a framework for guiding international economic relations would benefit from Soviet collaboration.[8] The same argument can be applied to Russia.

Of course, concern about weakening multilateralism is less relevant if one believes Russia will not realize its potential to become a major trading country until it completes the transition to a market-oriented system. But if one holds this belief, then consistency requires dismissing as irrelevant some of the concerns raised by trade policy officials who were opposed to Soviet participation in the GATT and may likewise oppose Russian participation until the country adopts an economic system compatible with the market-oriented rules of the international trade institution.

The trade policy implications of including the Soviet Union's successor states in the GATT are not, however, one-sided. One does need to consider seriously the possible negative consequences so often noted by Western governments in the 1980s. Countries like Russia and Ukraine have potentially large trading capabilities. In addition, as mentioned, the GATT is far more fragile today than it was at the time of the Polish, Rumanian, and Hungarian accessions. Further departures from the established market-oriented rules of the game could erode the institution's ability to provide a coherent framework for international trade. However, the severity of this threat, like the threat of bilateralism should Russia be excluded from the GATT, depends on whether Russia does indeed realize its potential to become a major trading country before completing the transition to a market-oriented system. If one believes that Russian trading capabilities will be limited until the process of economic reform is completed, then the potential damage that may be done to the cohesion of the GATT will be less severe.

The second main trade policy issue that poses a significant dilemma is the long-standing one of how to devise an entrance fee that simultaneously upholds reciprocity and nondiscrimination by the nonmarket country. The conventional procedure, tariff concessions, would not assure other GATT members of increased export opportunities. This issue was of much concern to the EC at the time of the Polish, Rumanian, and Hungarian accession negotiations. The concern is likely to be heightened in the Russian case, given the potentially large size of that country's trading capabilities. One may also expect that some American officials will join those in the EC who have traditionally focused on reciprocity, given the signs of shifts in U.S. trade policy away from nondiscrimination.

In summary, although there are strong reasons for adopting a favorable approach toward the new states' accession to the GATT, some serious problems also need to be addressed. Flexibility and pragmatism will therefore be required here, as in many other new challenges that have faced the GATT since its creation in 1947.

Olivier Long, former director-general of the GATT, has written that the institution has usually adopted a flexible and pragmatic approach to cope with change, new issues, and challenges. He has suggested that "had GATT law remained immutable, it would certainly have lost most of its authority. The adaptations and modifications that have been made should not be looked upon as evidence of weakness but rather as an indication of the viability of the system and of a willingness to change."[9] Change has occurred in the former Soviet Union and the world. If the GATT is to keep up, a flexible approach will be necessary.

Accession on Transitional Terms

Given the trade policy dilemmas raised by a nonmarket country's participation in the GATT, it is unrealistic to consider the possibility of accession by countries like Russia and Kazakhstan on the same terms of agreement as those accorded to market countries in the early 1990s. However strong the political will to aid the new sovereign states may be, Western governments are unlikely to accept such terms of agreement until these countries move much further toward a market economy. Such change will take some years. It is therefore more realistic to consider an option that will be referred to here as accession on transitional terms.

Accession on transitional terms would mean full membership in the GATT, but the terms of the agreement would differ from those accorded to market countries, as they did in the Polish, Hungarian, and Rumanian cases. However, unlike the arrangement in those cases, the protocols of accession for the Soviet Union's successor states would explicitly note that the terms of agreement were transitional or temporary.[10] The agreements could provide for annual or biennial reviews to oversee the implementation stage, as was done for other nonmarket countries, and it could be explicitly stated in the agreement that the reviews would consider the possibilities of renegotiating the terms of agreement in the future.

This proposal for accession on transitional terms would have several advantages. Making the terms transitional would reflect the situation in the countries of the former Soviet Union; it would provide an easy opening for renegotiating terms appropriate for a market country when an individual country reaches that stage; above all, it might eliminate some of the undiplomatic second-class-citizenship status that Poland, Rumania, and Hungary experienced.

ENTRANCE FEE. The transitional or temporary terms of agreement could depart from conventional protocols of accession in some ways to accommodate key problems posed by a nonmarket country's accession to the GATT. One of the most important is how to devise a suitable entrance fee. Ideally, the entrance fee should reflect diffuse reciprocity, to ensure that the applicant grants other GATT members both nondiscriminatory and increased market access. The applicant becomes entitled to two main benefits: the nondiscriminatory treatment theoretically associated with most-favored-nation status, and the increased market access associated with the lower tariff rates of most-favored-nation status. The applicant is also supposed to reciprocate these benefits.

The entrance fees devised for the Polish and Rumanian cases were a variant of the quantitative import commitment. But neither of these so-called solutions proved to be very satisfactory, and there appears to be a general consensus that the obligations had little or no impact on foreign trade decisions. Western governments have since made significant efforts to address the dilemmas in the context of the bilateral trade agreements reached with the Eastern countries in the post-cold-war world. They have refrained from adopting any variant of the quantitative import commitment and have instead focused on upholding nondiscrimination and promoting conditions conducive to the market mechanism. The obligations inserted in these recent bilateral agreements reflect diffuse reciprocity and are compatible with the GATT. Hence, there is little reason for not using similar solutions in a multilateral agreement between the Soviet Union's successor states and the GATT.

For example, the bilateral trade agreements that the EC and the United States negotiated with the Soviet Union in the post-cold-war world upheld nondiscrimination. The terms of the U.S.-Soviet agreement obliged the Soviet Union to do the following: to apply nondiscriminatory treatment with regard to quantitative restrictions, the granting of licenses, technical standards, business facilities, and the allocation of hard currency; to increasingly apply national treatment to foreign goods and services; and to increase transparency on its foreign trade regulations. In principle, the Soviet Union's successor states could undertake similar commitments upon accession to the GATT and thereby abide by GATT obligations. Problems of enforcement may be encountered, but such potential problems did not deter Western governments in bilateral agreements.

In addition, the bilateral trade agreements included what is referred to as the business clause, in order to uphold reciprocity. This clause aimed to ensure increased access to the Soviet market and foster conditions amenable to foreign business representatives. Specifically, the Soviet Union undertook to expand and improve opportunities for foreign business representatives in the USSR with regard to matters such as office and residential space, contacts with end users, transport facilities, and the recruitment of local staff. In principle, a similar clause could be inserted into a multilateral agreement between the successor states and the GATT to uphold reciprocity. In addition or as an alternative, the entrance fee employed in the Hungarian case (tariff concessions) could be used, although this might have little immediate effect on the nonmarket country's foreign trade decisions.

Some officials and observers in the West no doubt attach much importance to reciprocity. They could be dissatisfied with the terms of the recent bilateral agreements and be unwilling to incorporate similar terms into a multilateral agreement. They might consider that the business clause does not provide an adequate guarantee of increased export opportunities and that the Soviet Union's successor states should be required to undertake a quantitative import commitment upon accession to the GATT. This would be in addition to, or in place of, the business clause or tariff concessions. Many Western European representatives made similar suggestions when Hungary asked to join the GATT on the basis of tariff concessions in the early 1970s.

An entrance fee that uses a variant of the quantitative import commitment might provide increased export opportunities in the short run, providing that it is enforced. However, it would also have some deleterious consequences.

A quantitative import commitment would lock the nonmarket countries into an obligation devised for a planned-economy country and might therefore retard the process of economic reform. Hence, in the long run this clause could reduce market access by preventing the increased export opportunities that might arise if a business clause that encourages market-oriented reform were used instead. It was this desire to promote conditions conducive to economic reform that apparently led the U.S. government to omit any variant of the quantitative import commitment from the U.S.-Soviet bilateral trade agreement of 1990.[11] This consideration likewise contributed to the U.S. decision to support the Hungarian request that tariff concessions be accepted as a legitimate entrance fee in the early 1970s.

A quantitative import commitment also reflects specific reciprocity and would therefore pose a greater threat to the liberal orientation of GATT rules than would the inclusion of a business clause. Use of a quantitative commitment could open the path to further results-oriented, market-sharing agreements that similarly reflect specific reciprocity and undermine the market-oriented framework of the international trading system.

Finally, when discussing the issue of reciprocity, it is appropriate to remember that the Soviet Union's successor states may themselves gain few tangible benefits from GATT membership. The main tangible benefit is MFN treatment. Many countries granted the Soviet Union this in the context of bilateral agreements. If the same treatment is automatically extended to the successor states in the context of bilateral agreements, then opportunities for the applicants to increase their exports will change little upon accession to the GATT. One may therefore question why the applicants should themselves be expected to grant other countries significantly greater market access upon their accession to the GATT.

SAFEGUARDS. As often noted by the EC during its past disputes with Eastern countries, the possibility of heavily subsidized products from nonmarket countries could present contracting parties with a threat of market disruption. Although it is difficult to see how exports from the Soviet Union's successor states could threaten significant market disruption today, given the terrible state of these countries' economies, this situation could of course change.

The solution used in earlier cases involving nonmarket countries was to insert a discriminatory safeguard clause in the agreement that would allow contracting parties to block imports from the nonmarket country while continuing to import similar products from third countries. This solution obviously undermines the GATT norm of nondiscrimination, but it is a solution that the key contracting parties may present as a precondition for agreement. Even the United States, which generally championed nondiscrimination in the earlier negotiations with Poland, Rumania, and Hungary, favored inserting a discriminatory safeguard clause into their protocols of accession.[12]

In addition to the plentiful supply of safeguard mechanisms that are intended to be used for economic reasons, there is also an escape clause that can be used for political reasons should a contracting party have broader problems with the applicant's participation in the GATT. Any country that is very strongly opposed to the applicant's accession can invoke article 35 of the GATT, which permits the nonapplication of the General Agreement between two contracting parties if "either of the contracting parties, at the time either becomes a contracting party, does not consent to such application." The United States, which invoked article 35 when Rumania and Hungary joined, still maintains domestic legislation that would require it to invoke article 35 should nonmarket countries join the GATT. Moreover, although approval of a decision to grant an applicant membership in the GATT requires the consent of two-thirds of the contracting parties, it seems there is no constraint on the number of contracting parties that can invoke article 35. It appears that no contracting party voted against the decision to allow Japan to accede to the GATT in 1955, but many contracting parties then invoked article 35 (which they have since disinvoked) in the Japanese case.[13] In short, the GATT provides much scope for flexibility that can facilitate the task of accommodating accession by the sovereign states of the former Soviet Union.

Provisional Accession

A category known as provisional accession in GATT circles provides a possible alternative for nonmarket countries' participation in the GATT. This option has been used in other cases where specific problems were encountered—Yugoslavia, for example. It reflects the flexible and pragmatic approach taken in the GATT forum.[14] Provisional accession has often been applied when it was necessary to delay negotiating the tariff concessions expected from the applicant as its entrance fee to the GATT. In these circumstances the applicant provisionally accedes to the GATT until tariff concessions are negotiated, whereupon full accession occurs.

Provisional accession means that commercial relations between the signatories are conducted on the basis of the General Agreement. Two main differences distinguish provisional accession from full accession. First, provisional accession means that the agreement applies only to the country concerned and those contracting parties that choose to sign it. The agreement, like full accession, has to be approved by two-thirds of the contracting parties, but it is then technically sufficient if only one contracting party signs it. In contrast, under full accession the agreement automatically applies to all contracting parties, and any country that wants to opt out of the agreement has to invoke article 35. Second, under provisional accession the applicant's tariff rates are not bound, leaving the country free to alter the rates of duty, whereas under full accession the newcomer's tariff rates are bound at the agreed-upon level. Thus, under provisional accession those contracting parties that choose to sign the agreement are theoretically given the option of withdrawing tariff concessions from the applicant should the latter raise its tariff rates. However, in practice the route taken by a contracting party that is dissatisfied is simply not to sign the agreement, which is subject to periodic renewal.[15]

This option was the route chosen for Yugoslavia, whose request for provisional accession (under conventional terms employed for market countries) was approved in 1962. Full accession, on the same terms of agreement as those accorded to market countries, took place several years later, in 1966. The Yugoslav case, which focused on what can be termed a phased accession process, may provide an appropriate precedent for the Soviet Union's successor states. Full accession was deemed inappropriate in 1962 because Yugoslavia had not yet adopted a definitive customs tariff. Concerns about the tariff in the reforming nonmarket countries today could make provisional accession an appropriate option for the Soviet Union's successor states. But this option may be less suitable than the previously discussed option of accession on transitional terms. Apparently provisional accession has since become unpopular in GATT circles, largely because of experience with Tunisia, which maintained this status for many years even though hardly any contracting parties signed the agreement over time.[16] In addition, although one may question the objective economic rationale behind the decision to grant Yugoslavia terms of agreement identical to those accorded to market countries in the 1960s, it does not seem realistic to believe that key contracting parties will be willing to accord such countries as Russia similar terms of agreement for quite a few more years. The potentially large size of Russian trading capabilities may make contracting parties more cautious.

Conclusion

The world was left rather stunned by the events in Eastern Europe in 1989. Further shocks occurred in August 1991, when the dramatic events in the Soviet Union demonstrated the profound changes that had occurred in that country. Anyone who spent time in the Soviet Union in pre-perestroika years could not fail to be amazed at the scene of the crowds surrounding the Russian parliament in August 1991 and the subsequent uprooting of the statue of Feliks Dzerzhinsky, founder of the secret police. Change came to be expected as the norm, and by the end of December 1991 few people were surprised when the Soviet Union was itself dissolved. The changes that have occurred in the former Soviet Union since Gorbachev initiated the policy of perestroika in the mid-1980s are truly immense. The process of transformation clearly still has far to go, and setbacks may occur. But in the early 1990s few if any arguments can be found to exclude the reforming sovereign states of the former Soviet Union from the global community. On the contrary, the situation mandates that efforts be made to include these countries.

The need for a policy of inclusion, or positive engagement, was stated by the leaders of the world's seven main industrial economies at the G-7 summit in July 1991 and was reemphasized in January 1992 after the collapse of the Soviet Union. A logical extension of the policy of inclusion is to integrate the successor states into the main international trade institution of the global community. The task of integrating these countries into the GATT clearly poses a significant challenge and raises trade policy dilemmas that may elicit diverse and conflicting responses in the West. But the new political landscape of the post-cold-war world indicates that trade policy officials will be left with no choice but to consider seriously the task at hand and to adopt a flexible and pragmatic approach on the road to a global GATT.

Notes

A Note on Sources

In this study I use data derived from extensive interviews that I conducted with numerous former and current officials from the European Community (Commission, France, Germany, Great Britain, and the Netherlands), the GATT secretariat, Hungary, Poland, the United States (Commerce Department, Office of the U.S. Trade Representative, and State Department), and elsewhere. The interviews, which were undertaken between January 1986 and August 1991, were primarily conducted in Brussels, Budapest, Geneva, and Washington and were granted on the condition that I preserve the anonymity of the officials interviewed. In most cases, I was able to cross-check the material with at least three different former or current officials. When this was not possible, I have either omitted the material or introduced it with the words *apparently* or *it seems*. I have also relied on written documents to which I was granted access. Many U.S. documents were obtained through the Freedom of Information Act, which enabled me to quote them more extensively than other documents. The interviews used in this manuscript are numbered; the written documents are cited as U.S. notes, EC notes, and GATT documents.

Chapter 1

1. Although twenty-three countries negotiated the General Agreement, only twenty-two of these countries were original signatories. Chile was the exception, and was not an original signatory of the GATT.

2. De facto application of the GATT is an intermediary stage to full accession under article 26:5c for former colonies that have gained independence. It means that contracting parties apply de facto the General Agree-

ment to those former colonies which apply de facto the General Agreement to the contracting parties. As Kenneth Dam explains, de facto application is an example of the pragmatic approach taken in the GATT forum. It is a status that was not specifically authorized by the General Agreement, but represents an evolution in GATT practices in order to cope with issues that were not foreseen when the General Agreement was drafted. See Kenneth W. Dam, *The GATT: Law and International Economic Organization* (University of Chicago Press, 1970), pp. 346–47.

3. Technically, it is incorrect to use the term *member* because the GATT is not an organization but merely a multilateral treaty. The correct technical term is *contracting party*. However, because the GATT has taken on the role of an institution, *member* and *membership* are widely employed. See John Jackson, *The World Trading System: Law and Policy of International Economic Relations* (MIT Press, 1989), p. 45.

4. This book therefore does not analyze the case of Yugoslavia's accession to the GATT. Yugoslavia, unlike Poland, Rumania, and Hungary, acceded to the GATT on "normal" terms. In other words, Yugoslavia's protocol of accession to the GATT is the same as those of market countries, and does not include the discriminatory clauses that were inserted into the protocols of accession for Poland, Rumania and Hungary. The decision to omit the Yugoslav case is not meant to imply that the Yugoslav case bears no relevance to this study. It does, and the relevant points are referred to in the concluding chapter.

5. There were some specific differences in the nature of the applicants' economic systems. In particular, Hungary applied to join the GATT when it introduced the reform plan known as the new economic mechanism (NEM) in 1968. Nonetheless, as Janos Kornai has argued, the budget constraint under the NEM remained "basically rather soft", thus distinguishing it from a market system in which hard budget constraints prevail. See Janos Kornai, *Economics of Shortage* (Amsterdam: North-Holland Publishing Company, 1980), p. 314. Kornai explains, "The soft budget constraint—as opposed to the hard one—is unable to act as an effective behavioral constraint, but exists only as an accounting relationship" (p. 309).

6. *Wall Street Journal*, August 21, 1986.

7. "Soviet Asks to Attend GATT Meeting," *New York Times*, August 24, 1986, sec. 4, p. 2.

8. Jackson, *World Trading System*, p. 290. Jackson himself then briefly disputes the policy implications of this conventional argument.

9. One of the most scholarly works that focus heavily on more technical economic issues is Harriet Matejka, "Central Planning, Trade Policy Instruments and Centrally Planned Economies within the Framework of the General Agreement on Tariffs and Trade," *Journal of Development Planning*, vol. 20 (1990). The most thorough work on the subject of Eastern European relations with the GATT is Maciej M. Kostecki, *East-West Trade and the GATT System* (London: Macmillan for the Trade Policy Research Centre, 1979). Although Kostecki focuses on economic issues, he clearly acknowledges the

importance of broader political issues. For a more recent book that discusses the subject, see Jozef M. van Brabant, *The Planned Economies and International Economic Organizations* (Cambridge University Press, 1991). For a study that focuses on political rather than technical economic questions of a related subject, see Harold K. Jacobson and Michel Oksenberg, *China's Participation in the IMF, the World Bank, and GATT: Toward a Global Economic Order* (University of Michigan Press, 1990).

Chapter 2

1. Thomas A. Kalil, "The Uruguay Round: An Interview with Ambassador Michael B. Smith," *Fletcher Forum: A Journal of Studies in International Affairs*, vol. 11 (Winter 1987), p. 18.

2. For work on the intra-alliance politics of COCOM, see Michael Mastanduno, "Trade as a Strategic Weapon: American and Alliance Export Control Policy in the Early Postwar Period," *International Organization*, vol. 42 (Winter 1988), pp. 121–50; and Michael Mastanduno, "The Management of Alliance Export Control Policy: American Leadership and the Politics of COCOM," in Gary K. Bertsch, ed., *Controlling East-West Trade and Technology Transfer* (Duke University Press, 1988), pp. 241–79.

3. See Michael Mastanduno, "Strategies of Economic Containment: U.S. Trade Relations with the Soviet Union," *World Politics*, vol. 37 (July 1985), pp. 503–31; and John Lewis Gaddis, *Strategies of Containment: A Critical Appraisal of Postwar American National Security Policy* (Oxford University Press, 1982).

4. The Trade Agreements Extension Act of 1951 obligated the president to suspend, withdraw, or prevent the application of most-favored-nation treatment to "imports from the Union of Soviet Socialist Republics and to imports from any nation or area dominated or controlled by the foreign government or foreign organization controlling the world Communist movement." See *East-West Trade*, Hearings before the Senate Committee on Foreign Relations, 89 Cong. 1 sess. (Government Printing Office, 1965), pt. 2, p. 274. Products from the East thus became subject to the prohibitively high rates of duty established in the 1930 Smoot-Hawley Act.

5. As Mastanduno explains, the strategy of economic warfare assumed there was an indirect link between trade and military capabilities. It was based on the belief that trade would increase the quantity of resources available in the Soviet Union and that these gains from trade would in turn be channeled into the military sector. Hence, it was presumed that trade would indirectly increase Soviet military power and thus constituted a threat to American national security. All trade with the Soviet Union was therefore to be prohibited. See Mastanduno, "Strategies of Economic Containment," pp. 506–10.

6. Gaddis, *Strategies of Containment*, p. 289.

7. A U.S.-Soviet bilateral trade agreement, which provided for the mutual granting of MFN status, was signed in October 1972. However, it never

came into force. The Jackson-Vanik amendment, which was incorporated into the 1974 Trade Act, prevented the United States from fulfilling its commitments under the terms of the bilateral trade agreement, which required the granting of MFN status, and the Soviet Union consequently renounced the agreement. For a detailed account of the domestic politics behind the Jackson-Vanik amendment, see Paula Stern, *Water's Edge: Domestic Politics and the Making of American Foreign Policy* (Westport, Conn.: Greenwood Press, 1979).

8. For more details on French policy toward the Soviet Union, see Pierre Hassner, "France and the Soviet Union," in Michael Mandelbaum, ed., *Western Approaches to the Soviet Union* (New York: Council on Foreign Relations, 1988), pp. 25–51; Edward A. Kolodziej, *French International Policy under De Gaulle and Pompidou: The Politics of Grandeur* (Cornell University Press, 1974); and Marie-Hélène Labbé, "Controlling East-West Trade in France," in Bertsch, ed., *Controlling East-West Trade*, pp. 183–203.

9. For more details on West Germany's policy toward the Soviet Union, see Hans-Dietrich Genscher, "Toward an Overall Western Strategy for Peace, Freedom and Progress," *Foreign Affairs*, vol. 61 (Fall 1982), pp. 42–66; and Hanns-Dieter Jacobsen, "East-West Trade and Export Controls: The West German Perspective," in Bertsch, ed., *Controlling East-West Trade*, pp. 159–82.

10. For more details on British poilicy toward the Soviet Union, see Gary Bertsch and Steven Elliot, "Controlling East-West Trade in Britain: Power, Politics, and Policy," in Bertsch, ed., *Controlling East-West Trade*, pp. 204–40; and Stephen Woolcock, "Great Britain," in Reinhard Rode and Hanns-Dieter Jacobsen, eds., *Economic Warfare or Detente: An Assessment of East-West Relations in the 1980's* (Boulder, Colo.: Westview Press, 1985), pp. 141–56.

11. Bruce W. Jentleson, *Pipeline Politics: The Complex Political Economy of East-West Energy Trade* (Cornell University Press, 1986).

12. For more details on U.S. policy toward Eastern Europe, see Raymond L. Garthoff, "Eastern Europe in the Context of U.S.-Soviet Relations," in Sarah Meiklejohn Terry, ed., *Soviet Policy in Eastern Europe* (Council on Foreign Relations, and Yale University Press, 1984); and Lincoln Gordon, "Interests and Policies in Eastern Europe: The View from Washington," in Lincoln Gordon and others, *Eroding Empire: Western Relations with Eastern Europe* (Brookings, 1987), pp. 67–128.

13. Gunnar Adler-Karlsson, *Western Economic Warfare: 1947–1967: A Case Study in Foreign Economic Policy* (Stockholm: Almqvist and Wiksell, 1968), pp. 99–100.

14. *East-West Trade*, Hearings, pt. 2, pp. 274–76.

15. Adler-Karlsson, *Western Economic Warfare*, p. 103.

16. Pierre Hassner, "The View from Paris," in Gordon and others, *Eroding Empire*, pp. 189–231.

17. Josef Joffe, "The View from Bonn: The Tacit Alliance," in Gordon and others, *Eroding Empire*, pp. 129–87.

18. Richard N. Gardner, *Sterling-Dollar Diplomacy in Current Perspective: The Origins and the Prospects of Our International Economic Order* (Columbia University Press, 1980), p. 379.

19. The following trade rounds have been completed: Geneva 1947; Annecy 1949; Torquay 1951; Geneva 1956; Geneva 1960–61 (known as the Dillon Round); Geneva 1964–67 (known as the Kennedy Round); Geneva 1973–79 (known as the Tokyo Round). See Olivier Long, *Law and Its Limitations in the GATT Multilateral Trade System* (Dordrecht: Martinus-Nijhoff, 1985), p. 22.

20. Jackson, *World Trading System*, p. 53.

21. Quantitative restrictions involve greater intervention in the market mechanism than tariffs do because they literally seal off the domestic market from imported goods beyond the specified quantity. Foreign producers cannot increase their penetration of the domestic market even if they increase their efficiency relative to that of domestic producers. Tariffs divorce the domestic price from the world market price and increase the domestic price of the imported good by the rate of the duty applied. However, foreign suppliers are not literally banned from the domestic market if a tariff is applied. Foreign producers may therefore increase their penetration of the domestic market if they increase their efficiency relative to that of domestic producers. Furthermore, quantitative restrictions are less transparent than tariffs and are often allocated in a manner that allows for discrimination.

22. Gerard Curzon and Victoria Curzon, "Non-Discrimination and the Rise of Material Reciprocity," *World Economy*, vol. 12 (December 1989), p. 482.

23. Robert O. Keohane, "Reciprocity in International Relations," *International Organization*, vol. 40 (Winter 1986), p. 4.

24. See Keohane, "Reciprocity in International Relations," pp. 16–17.

25. Curzon and Curzon, "Non-Discrimination and the Rise of Material Reciprocity," pp. 487–89.

26. For a discussion on the pros and cons of various practices that are often labeled as managed trade, see Robert Z. Lawrence and Charles L. Schultze, eds., *An American Trade Srategy: Options for the 1990s* (Brookings, 1990).

27. See Long, *Law and Its Limitations*.

28. For an analysis of these negotiations during the Tokyo Round, see Gilbert R. Winham, *International Trade and the Tokyo Round Negotiation* (Princeton University Press, 1987).

29. For explanations of planned economic systems, see Franklyn D. Holzman, *Foreign Trade under Central Planning* (Harvard University Press, 1974); and Janos Kornai, *Economics of Shortage* (Amsterdam: North Holland, 1980).

30. In addition, nontariff elements of applicants' trade policies have been increasingly examined in accession negotiations. See Long, *Law and Its Limitations*, pp. 36–40.

31. Martin Domke and John N. Hazard, "State Trading and the Most-Favored Nation Clause," *American Journal of International Law*, vol. 50 (January

1958), pp. 56–57.

32. Domke and Hazard, "State Trading and the Most-Favored Nation Clause," p. 59.

Chapter 3

1. See Karen Dawisha, *Eastern Europe, Gorbachev and Reform: The Great Challenge* (Cambridge University Press, 1990), chap. 4.

2. Interview 18.

3. U.S. note, February 21, 1967, p. 8.

4. J. Woznowski, "The Socialist Countries' Membership in the GATT," *Polish Yearbook of International Law*, 1970, p. 205.

5. M. M. Kostecki, *East-West Trade and the GATT System* (London: Macmillan for the Trade Policy Research Centre, 1979), p. 27.

6. GATT documents L/967 and L/1049.

7. Interviews 5 and 18; and EC note, November 23, 1979.

8. Interview 100.

9. Interview 98.

10. Interviews 2, 8, and 18.

11. Woznowski, "Socialist Countries' Membership," p. 211.

12. Interviews 2, 8, and 18; Summary of statement by Polish representative at a working party meeting in January 1967, in U.S. note, February 21, 1967; and Woznowski, "Socialist Countries' Membership," p. 212.

13. GATT document L/1120.

14. Interviews 5, 18, 72, and 89; and Kostecki, *East-West Trade*, p. 29.

15. Interview 89.

16. "Looking Outwards," address by Eric Wyndham White, delivered before the General Export Association of Sweden, Stockholm, April 6, 1960, pp. 10–11.

17. "GATT as an International Trade Organization", address by Eric Wyndham White, delivered in Warsaw, June 1961, p. 29.

18. Interviews 10, 17, 18, 72, and 87.

19. For more details on the negotiations over Poland's participation in the Kennedy Round, see Bohdan Laczkowski, "Poland's Participation in the Kennedy Round," in Frans A. M. Alting Von Geusau, ed., *Economic Relations after The Kennedy Round* (Tilburg, Netherlands: A. W. Sijthoff-Leyden, 1969), pp. 83–93.

20. GATT document C/M/38.

21. U.S. note, January 19, 1967, pp. 3, 10, 11.

22. Interview 105.

23. Interviews 29, 30, 38, 100, 118, and 123.

24. Interviews 4, 5, 23, 28, 88, 96, 100, 110, and 120.

25. John Pinder and Pauline Pinder, *The European Community's Policy towards Eastern Europe* (London: Chatham House, 1975), p. 19.

26. Kenneth W. Dam, *The GATT: Law and International Economic Organization* (University of Chicago Press, 1970), p. 148.

27. Gardner Patterson, *Discrimination in International Trade: The Policy Issues, 1945–1965* (Princeton University Press, 1966), p. 24.

28. Interview 72.

29. U.S. note, March 1, 1967, pp. 1–2.

30. U.S. note, April 17, 1967.

31. U.S. notes, March 23, 1967, April 20, 1967, and June 6, 1967.

32. U.S. note, March 1, 1967.

33. U.S. note, March 7, 1967, p. 1.

34. U.S. note, June 6, 1967.

35. U.S. notes, June 6, 1967, and June 15, 1967.

36. The clause that was finally agreed upon and inserted in Poland's protocol of accession stated:

a) Contracting parties which on the date of this Protocol apply to imports from Poland prohibitions or quantitative restrictions which are inconsistent with Article XIII of the General Agreement may, notwithstanding these provisions, continue to apply such prohibitions or restrictions to their imports from Poland *provided* that the discriminatory element in these restrictions is (a) not increased and (b) progressively relaxed as far as the quantities or values of permitted imports of Polish origin are concerned so that at the expiry of the transitional period the length of which will be determined in accordance with (c) below, any inconsistency with the provisions of Article XIII has thus been eliminated.

b) The CONTRACTING PARTIES shall in the course of the annual consultations provided for in paragraph 5 below review measures taken by contracting parties pursuant to the provisions of this paragraph, and make such recommendations as they consider appropriate.

c) During the course of the third annual consultation provided for in paragraph 5 below, the CONTRACTING PARTIES shall, in the light of all relevant circumstances, consider the establishment of a date for the termination of the transitional period referred to in (a) above. If no such date is fixed during the course of such consultation, this question shall be re-examined at each subsequent annual consultation until a date is fixed.

A copy of the Polish protocol of accession can be found in Contracting Parties to the General Agreement on Tariffs and Trade, *Basic Instruments and Selected Documents*, 15th Supplement (Geneva: GATT, 1968), pp. 47–48.

37. U.S. note, February 23, 1967.

38. U.S. note, March 1, 1967.

39. Interview 72.

40. Kostecki, *East-West Trade*, p. 30.

41. A copy of the letter of application can be found in GATT document L/3050.

42. GATT document C/M/51, p. 3.

43. GATT documents Spec(69)86 and Spec(69)110.

44. Interviews 2, 5, 10, 18, 27, 72, and 87.

45. Interviews 2, 72, 87, and 91.

46. Henry Kissinger, *White House Years* (Little, Brown, 1979), pp. 155–58.
47. Interview 72.
48. Interview 91.
49. GATT document Spec(69)86.
50. EC note, April 11, 1969.
51. Interviews 91, 98, and 108.
52. Interviews 91, 98, and 108.
53. Poland had been granted MFN status in 1960, but the terms of the 1962 legislation (which differed from the terms of the prior legislation drawn up in 1951) technically required withdrawing this privilege from Poland. The terms of the 1962 legislation were therefore subsequently modified in the Foreign Assistance Act of 1963, which allowed the president to continue the extension of MFN treatment to a country that was already granted this status when the 1962 act was passed. See *East-West Trade*, Hearings before the Senate Committee on Foreign Relations, 89 Cong. 1 sess. (Government Printing Office, 1965), pt. 2, pp. 274–76.
54. EC note, December 3, 1969.
55. Interviews 72, 91, and 98.
56. EC notes, December 17, 1969, and April 14, 1970.
57. EC notes, December 17, 1969, April 14, 1970, and July 12, 1971.
58. Interviews 96, 97, 137, and 138.
59. EC notes, December 17, 1969, and July 17, 1971.
60. EC note, July 12, 1971.
61. EC note, July 12, 1971.
62. The approval by the Benelux governments was given on the condition that the EC Council minutes include a declaration that the burden of obligation to remove discriminatory QRs during the implementation phase would not fall disproportionately on certain member states. EC notes, July 17, 1971, and July 21, 1971. The clause that was inserted into the Rumanian protocol of accession stated:

3 (a) Contracting parties still maintaining prohibitions or quantitative restrictions not consistent with Article XIII of the General Agreement shall not increase the discriminatory element in these restrictions, undertake to remove them progressively and shall have as their objective to eliminate them before the end of 1974. Should this agreed objective not be achieved and, for exceptional reasons, should a limited number of restrictions still be in force as of 1 January 1975, the Working Party provided for in paragraph 5 would examine them with a view to their elimination.

(b) Contracting parties shall notify, on entry into force of this Protocol, and before the consultations provided for in paragraph 5 below, discriminatory prohibitions and quantitative restrictions still applied at that time to imports from Romania. Such notifications shall include a list of the products subject to these prohibitions and restrictions, specifying the type of restrictions applied (import quotas, licensing systems, embargoes, etc.) as well as the value of trade effected in the products concerned and the measures adopted with a view to eliminating these prohibitions and restrictions under the terms of the preceding sub-paragraph.

(c) The CONTRACTING PARTIES shall, in the course of the consultations provided for in paragraph 5 below, review the measures taken or envisaged by contracting parties pursuant to the provisions of this paragraph, and make such recommendations as they consider appropriate. A copy of the Rumanian protocol of accession can be found in Contracting Parties to the General Agreement on Tariffs and Trade, *Basic Instruments and Selected Documents*, 18th Supplement (Geneva: GATT, 1972), pp. 5–10.

63. GATT documents L/3211 and Spec(69)86.

64. Interview 32.

65. EC notes, December 3, 1969, and November 8, 1971.

66. EC notes, April 11, 1969, and December 3, 1969.

67. Contracting Parties to GATT, *Basic Instruments*, 18th Supp., p. 10.

68. Kostecki, *East-West Trade*, p. 31.

69. For more details, see J. F. Brown, *Eastern Europe and Communist Rule* (Duke University Press, 1988), chap. 6.

70. Tamas Bauer, "The Hungarian Alternative to Soviet-Type Planning," *Journal of Comparative Economics*, vol. 7 (September 1983), p. 312.

71. GATT document C/M/37.

72. Interview 88.

73. GATT document W24/8; and Hungary's Memorandum of Foreign Trade Regime, December 1969, p. 6.

74. GATT document W24/8, p. 3.

75. EC notes, April 18, 1969, and July 8, 1969.

76. GATT document C/M/56.

77. GATT document Spec(70)83, p. 7.

78. U.S. note, March 1, 1971.

79. Calculated from data in International Monetary Fund, *Direction of Trade Annual, 1968–1972* (Washington, 1973).

80. Interviews 13, 18, 29, and 72.

81. Interviews 8, 64, 72, 87, and 91.

82. Interviews 64 and 91.

83. U.S. note, March 6, 1972, pp. 1–2.

84. U.S. note, November 12, 1971; and Interview 98.

85. U.S. note, June 14, 1971.

86. Interviews 10, 18, 26, 29, 87, and 108.

87. U.S. note, March 1, 1971; and Interview 61.

88. Interview 108.

89. GATT document Spec(71)1, pp. 12–13.

90. Interview 29; and U.S. note, November 12, 1971. The clause inserted into the Hungarian protocol of accession stated:

3 (a) Paragraph 1 shall not prevent the maintenance by Hungary of its existing trading regulations with respect to products originating in or destined for the countries enumerated in Annex A hereto.

(b) Hungary undertakes that her trading regulations or any change in them, or any extension of the list of countries referred to in the previous sub-paragraph shall not impair her commitments, discriminate against or otherwise operate to the detriment of contracting parties.

The following countries were listed in annex A: Albania, Bulgaria, Czechoslovakia, the German Democratic Republic, the Democratic People's Republic of Korea, Mongolia, the People's Republic of China, Poland, Romania, the Union of Soviet Socialist Republics, the Democratic Republic of Viet-Nam.

A copy of the Hungarian protocol of accession can be found in Contracting Parties to the General Agreement on Tariff and Trade, *Basic Instruments and Selected Documents*, 20th Supplement (Geneva: GATT, 1974), pp. 3–8.

91. U.S. note, July 21, 1972.

92. U.S. note, March 1, 1971.

93. EC notes, November 18, 1971, and February 4, 1972.

94. EC notes, November 18, 1971, and February 4, 1972; and U.S. note, November 12, 1971.

95. U.S. notes, March 6, 1972, June 12, 1972, and July 21, 1972. The final agreement was somewhat ambiguously phrased:

a) Contracting parties still maintaining prohibitions or quantitative restrictions not consistent with Article XIII of the General Agreement on imports from Hungary shall not increase the discriminatory element in these restrictions and undertake to remove them progressively.

b) If, for exceptional reasons, any such prohibitions or restrictions are still in force as of 1 January 1975, the Working Party provided for in paragraph 6 will examine them with a view to their elimination.

c) To this end, contracting parties shall notify, on entry into force of this Protocol, on 1 January 1975, and thereafter before the consultations provided for in paragraph 6 below, discriminatory prohibitions and quantitative restrictions still applied to imports from Hungary. Such notifications shall include a list of the products subject to these prohibitions and restrictions, specifying the type of restrictions applied (import quotas, licensing systems, embargoes, etc.) as well as the value of trade effected in the products concerned and the measures adopted with a view to eliminating these prohibitions and restrictions under the terms of the preceding sub-paragraphs.

Contracting Parties to GATT, *Basic Instruments*, 20th Supp., p. 4.

96. Interviews 54 and 61; and U.S. note, March 6, 1972.

97. U.S. note, March 1, 1971; and GATT document Spec(72)83.

Chapter 4

1. Poland's protocol of accession to the GATT specified that there were to be annual consultations to oversee the implementation of the accord, whereas the Rumanian and Hungarian protocols of accession specified that the reviews were to be held biennially.

2. The question of establishing a date for the termination of the transitional period was raised at the third consultation held in 1970, but it turned out to be impossible to reach an agreement. The subject was addressed at all subsequent consultations, debates were held, and no concrete results were obtained.

3. GATT document L/3577/Add. 3.

4. GATT document L/3597.

5. GATT documents L/3743/Add. 2. and L/3751.

6. GATT document L/3751.

7. For more details on the reviews of the Polish protocol, see GATT documents L/3093, L/3315, L/3475, L/3597, L/3751, L/3946, L/4096, L/4237, and L/4483. For more details on the reviews of the Rumanian protocol, see GATT documents L/3875, L/4469, L/5046, L/5464, L/5856, and L/6282. For more details on the reviews of the Hungarian protocol, see GATT documents L/4228, L/4633, L/4930, L/5303, L/5635, and L/5977.

8. This figure was questioned by the EC representative, who maintained that the correct sum was less than 8 percent. In addition, according to the Rumanian delegation, Sweden applied discriminatory restrictions against 3 percent of its imports from Rumania (mainly in textiles), and Norway applied discriminatory restrictions against 2 percent of its imports from Rumania in 1980. See GATT document L/5046. Finland applied discriminatory restrictions against 15 percent of its imports from Rumania in 1980. These were all removed on January 1, 1982. See GATT document L/5464.

9. Interviews 39, 53, and 101.

10. GATT document L/5977.

11. See Janos Martonyi, "Eastern European Countries and the GATT," in Marc Maresceau, ed., *The Political and Legal Framework of Trade Relations Between the European Community and Eastern Europe* (Dordrecht, Netherlands: Martinus-Nijhoff, 1989), p. 282.

12. General Agreement on Tariffs and Trade, *Trade Policy Review: Hungary*, vol. 1 (Geneva: GATT, 1991), pp. 135–36.

13. Interview 112. In the biennual GATT reviews during the implementation stage, as in the earlier negotiations over terms of agreement, the United States gave Hungary substantial support, upholding the GATT rule of nondiscrimination and advocating the honoring of commitments. Outside the GATT forum, however, the United States generally abstained from actively intervening in support of Hungary or the other socialist countries during the implementation stage. Many officials attributed this to American unwillingness to let the issue of QRs antagonize relations with its Western allies. In short, the trade policy alliance between the United States and Hungary was dampened by the trade policy gap between nonmarket systems and the GATT, and also by the security alliance between the United States and Western Europe. Interviews 40, 72, 83, 112, 113, and 123.

14. The increased pressure was most evident in the Hungarian case, for a variety of reasons. The Hungarian delegation pursued the matter most actively and could make a stronger case for removal than either Rumania

or Poland because its entrance fee (tariff concessions) left the Community with little opportunity to turn the tables and question whether the opponent was fulfilling its own commitment. The Polish delegation had the least power to pursue the issue, because of Poland's failure to fulfill its commitment after 1978. The reviews of the Polish protocol had subsequently been suspended, leaving Polish officials with little opportunity to pursue the fight over QRs.

15. Sweden and Norway removed their QRs when the Hungarian government indicated that it would be willing to undertake self- restraint measures under the special safeguard mechanism embodied in clause five of the Hungarian protocol of accession to the GATT. In other words, the restrictions were switched from QRs that were prohibited under clause four to self-restraint measures that were permitted under clause five. Thus Hungary obtained little increased export opportunities. But it obtained political benefits because the move left the EC completely isolated. The move also served to undermine the EC's argument that the Hungarian system of price formation constituted a permanent threat. Hungary provided evidence, by respecting the self-restraint measures with Sweden and Norway, to support the counterargument that ample safeguards existed in case of threat. A further side benefit from the agreements with Sweden and Norway was that the restrictions became temporary measures that were subject to annual bilateral agreements. Interviews 53, 54, 61, 65, and 69.

16. At the sixth review, held in 1986, the American representative stated that progress on removal of the QRs was too slow and that the date for complete elimination laid down in paragraph four of the agreement was long past. Similar sentiments were firmly expressed by others. Both the Japanese and Canadian representatives noted concern over the maintenance of discriminatory QRs twelve years after Hungary's accession to the GATT, and the Australian representative stressed that it was incumbent on contracting parties that maintained discriminatory measures to explain the "exceptional reasons." See GATT document L/5977.

17. GATT documents L/5303 and L/5977; and Interviews 28, 35, 36, 39, 53, and 54.

18. Interviews 99, 103, 105, and 107.

19. Interview 99.

20. Interviews 39, 61, 92, and 93.

21. Interview 93.

22. Agreement between the European Economic Community and the Socialist Republic of Romania on Trade in Industrial Products, *Official Journal of the European Community*, L/352, vol. 29 (December 1980).

23. Interviews 40, 64, 83, and 99.

24. Interview 83.

25. Interview 112.

26. GATT document L/5046; and Interviews 99, 103, and 104.

27. GATT documents L/3475, L/3597, L/3751, L/3946, L/4096, L/4237, and L/4483.

28. Ake Linden, "Relations between CMEA Countries and the GATT," in Gary Bertsch and Christopher Saunders, eds., *East-West Economic Relations in the 1990s* (London: Macmillan, 1990), p. 176.

29. GATT documents L/4469 and L/5046.

30. GATT documents L/5464 and L/6282.

31. GATT documents L/4228, L/4633, L/4930, L/5303, L/5635, and L/5977.

32. The Community meanwhile adopted what was known as the autonomous trade policy. The EC unilaterally extended de facto MFN status in tariff matters to products from the East. The absence of a legal framework to guide the conduct of trade was mitigated by the fact that the EC states evaded the Community policy that prohibited the conclusion of "trade agreements" between the member states and third countries by concluding so-called cooperation agreements with the Eastern European countries.

33. For more details on the history of the EC's relations with Eastern Europe, see Werner Feld, "The CMEA and the European Community: A Troubled Courtship," *Journal of European Integration*, vol 7, nos. 2–3 (1984); Peter Marsh, "The Development of Relations between the EEC and the CMEA," in Avi Shlaim and G. N. Yannopoulos, eds., *The EEC and Eastern Europe* (Cambridge University Press, 1978); John Maslen, "The European Community's Relations with the State-Trading Countries: 1981–1983," *Yearbook of European Law, 1984*; and John Maslen, "The European Community's Relations with the State-Trading Countries of Europe 1984–1986," *Yearbook of European Law, 1987*; John Pinder and Pauline Pinder, *The European Community's Policy towards Eastern Europe* (London: Chatham House, 1975); and John Pinder, "A Community Policy towards Eastern Europe," *World Today*, March 1974.

34. Peter Balazs, "Trade Relations between Hungary and the European Community," in Maresceau, ed., *Political and Legal Framework*, p. 65.

35. Interviews 92, 93, and 97; and *Europe*, June 15, 1988, p. 6.

36. Interviews 114, 116, 117, 118, 120, 122, and 123.

37. Interviews 34, 68, 88, 93, and 114.

38. Interviews 114, 122, and 123. The change in the EC states' position was also influenced by the aim of creating a single market by 1992. This goal required either the harmonization of the national QR lists or the elimination of the QRs—a goal that had some influence over the Commission's approach since the 1960s. The 1992 deadline provided officials from both the Commission and Hungary with increased leverage during their battle with the member states. The 1992 deadline did apparently contribute to the national governments' willingness to adopt a more open-minded approach to the problem. Interviews 92, 93, 95, 97, 101, 106, 107, and 110.

39. Agreement between the European Economic Community and the Hungarian People's Republic on Trade and Commercial Cooperation, *Official Journal of the European Communities*, L 327, vol. 31, (November 30, 1988); EC Press Release IP(88)419, July 1, 1988; and *Europe*, July 2, 1988, pp. 9–10.

40. GATT document C/RM/S/10A, p. 47. The EC-Soviet bilateral trade

and cooperation agreement of December 1989 provides for the elimination of all discriminatory QRs by December 1995, except for a limited number of products deemed particularly sensitive.

41. The agreements with Bulgaria and the Soviet Union were pending in Congress in mid-1991.

42. GATT/AIR/3199.

43. There was initially some delay because of disagreement over the terms of reference for a working party. The Hungarian government wanted very specific terms of reference that would enable it to merely delete the specific, unusual clauses from its existing protocol without negotiating an entirely new protocol. In contrast, the United States considered that such specific terms would prejudge the outcome of the negotiations and instead favored the same general terms of reference as those agreed upon in the Polish case. Interviews 146, 150, 151, and 153.

44. GATT document L/6862, p. 2; and Interviews 146, 149, 150, 151, 153.

45. As noted in chapter 3, domestic legislation prohibited the United States from extending MFN treatment to Hungary and Rumania when they joined the GATT, and the United States therefore invoked article 35. Subsequent legislation had permitted granting these two countries temporary, but not permanent, MFN status, and the United States had therefore failed to disinvoke article 35 of the GATT even though it extended (temporary) MFN status to Rumania and Hungary in 1975 and 1978, respectively.

46. Bulgaria, Rumania, and the Soviet Union remain subject to the application of title IV, and Poland has always been considered exempt.

Chapter 5

1. GATT document C/M/41.

2. In line with this approach the Bulgarian government made an unusual move by submitting a list of tariff concessions at the end of the Tokyo Round, and informing the secretariat that it would extend these concessions to imports from those countries that would grant tariff concessions to Bulgarian products, and that it would expect these concessions to be taken into full consideration should Bulgaria later enter into formal negotiations over accession to the GATT. GATT document MTN/TAR/10.

3. The Bulgarian government, when meeting with two GATT secretariat representatives in Sofia in October 1980, said that conversations with some EC member states had been fairly encouraging. The secretariat representatives forewarned, however, that the Commission's response was likely to be more negative.

4. The Commission informed Bulgaria that its initiatives were "welcomed," but tariff concessions did not constitute a basis for negotiation until Bulgaria provided proof that its tariff played a meaningful role. Clear access to the Bulgarian market would be expected in exchange for any obligations that the EC might undertake should Bulgaria join the GATT. EC note, April

22, 1980.

5. EC note, April 22, 1980.

6. EC note, November 23, 1979.

7. Copies of the Arrangement Regarding Bovine Meat and the International Dairy Arrangement can be found in Contracting Parties to the General Agreement on Tariffs and Trade, *Basic Instruments and Selected Documents*, 26th Supplement (Geneva: GATT, 1980), pp. 84–115.

8. EC note, August 1, 1980.

9. GATT document TBT/2.

10. Interview 3.

11. Gilbert R. Winham, *International Trade and the Tokyo Round Negotiation* (Princeton University Press, 1986), p. 195.

12. Winham, *International Trade*, p. 197.

13. Interview 40.

14. Interview 81.

15. The Bulgarian representative had suggested that the application should instead be discussed by the code's committee, which he regarded as competent to consider appropriate conditions for accession. The proposal to set up a working party had received a mixed response from other representatives. The Community and Canada both considered that a working party should be established to thoroughly examine relevant aspects of the Bulgarian system. However, delegates from other countries adopted a somewhat less firm stance. EC notes, October 17, 1980, and November 11, 1980.

16. GATT document TBT/7.

17. EC note, August 1, 1980; and Interviews 95 and 100.

18. Interviews 11, 33, and 36.

19. GATT document TBT/7; and Interviews 11, 14, and 54.

20. EC note, March 9, 1981.

21. EC note, March 9, 1981.

22. EC note, December 5, 1980; and Interview 95.

23. EC note, May 7, 1981.

24. Interview 81.

25. Winham, *International Trade*, pp. 197–200, 240–47.

26. EC notes, October 10, 1980, November 11, 1980, December 5, 1980, May 7, 1981, and May 8, 1981.

27. EC note, May 8, 1981; and Interview 67.

28. EC note, November 11, 1980.

29. EC notes, May 7, 1981, and May 8, 1981.

30. Interview 81.

31. Interviews 11, 33, 37, 40, 76, and 78.

32. Interview 81.

33. Interviews 3, 11, and 81.

34. Interview 81.

35. Interviews 33, 36, 37, 64, 71, and 81.

36. GATT document TBT/9.

37. GATT document TBT/9; and Interview 14.

38. Interviews 67 and 81.

39. Interviews 33, 42, 81, and 90.

40. Interviews 81, 82, and 100.

41. Interview 81.

42. GATT document L/6023.

43. Interviews 28, 29, 36, 37, 42, 78, and 127.

44. A copy of the ministerial declaration on the Uruguay Round can be found in Contracting Parties to the General Agreement on Tariffs and Trade, *Basic Instruments and Selected Documents*, 33d Supplement (Geneva: GATT, 1987), pp. 19–27.

45. The ministerial declaration of November 14, 1973, which had launched the Tokyo Round, stated that "the Ministers agree that it will be open to any other government, through a notification to the director-general, to participate in the negotiations. The Ministers hope that the negotiations will involve the active participation of as many countries as possible." Contracting Parties to the General Agreement on Tariffs and Trade, *Basic Instruments and Selected Documents*, 20th Supplement (Geneva: GATT, 1974), p. 20.

46. Margaret Chapman, ed., *Proceedings of an International Conference on "USSR Participation in the General Agreement on Tariffs and Trade (GATT)"* (Washington: American Committee on U.S.-Soviet Relations, 1989), p. 20; William L. Richter, "Soviet 'Participation' in GATT: A Case for Accession," *New York University Journal of International Law and Politics*, vol. 20 (Winter 1988), pp. 497–98; and Interview 104.

47. Interviews 32 and 33. It is also relevant to note that in 1981 most of the EC member states had apparently been willing in principle to extend tariff concessions to Bulgaria as a developing country, under the generalized system of preferences. EC note, September 30, 1981.

48. Interviews 32 and 42.

49. Interviews 106, 107, 108, 109, and 112.

50. Interviews 23, 32, 67, 94, and 95.

51. Interviews 71, 76, 77, 79, and 83.

52. Interviews 83 and 89.

53. Interviews 104 and 107.

54. See papers and statements presented by A. Guinev, A. Paparizov, and A. Yankov at the International Law Institute conference on Bulgaria and the GATT, Washington, September 14–15, 1987.

55. Interviews 23, 79, 107, and 110.

56. Interviews 132 and 135.

57. Interviews 139 and 142.

58. Interviews 115, 132, 135, 136, 137, and 142.

59. Interview 142.

60. Interviews 132, 135, 144, and 145. The compromise text on terms of reference was approved at a council meeting later that month, and a chair for the working party was agreed upon in the early summer of 1990.

61. Interviews 144 and 145; and *New York Times*, February 11, 1990, p. A20.

62. Interviews 150 and 153.

63. Interview 137.

Chapter 6

1. The Soviet Union abstained from attending the conferences where the draft charters for the ITO were discussed, and the global import commitment was subsequently omitted from the final Havana Charter for the ITO. A copy of the Suggested Charter for an International Trade Organization can be found in U.S. Department of State, *Commercial Policy Series*, no. 93 (1946).

2. Cited in Paul Marer, "Growing Soviet International Economic Isolation," *PlanEcon Report*, vol. 11 (July 31, 1986), p. 6; see also John Lewis Gaddis, *The United States and the Origins of the Cold War, 1941–1947* (Columbia University Press, 1972), p. 22.

3. Raymond F. Mikesell, "Negotiating at Bretton Woods, 1944," in Raymond Dennett and Joseph E. Johnson, eds., *Negotiating with the Russians* (World Peace Foundation, 1951), pp. 101–06; and Valerie J. Assetto, *The Soviet Bloc in the IMF and the IBRD* (Boulder, Colo.: Westview Press, 1988), pp. 56–63.

4. Interview 132.

5. For more details on institutional practices regarding observer status, see GATT document C/173. Effective January 1, 1989, observer governments were also expected to pay a small fee toward the cost of documentation services.

6. Interview 8. It was not possible to determine whether the proposal to draft criteria for obtaining observer status was *initially* influenced by the Soviet approaches.

7. Interviews 26, 40, 64, 78, and 132. In the meantime applications from other governments were likewise apparently technically denied but in essence granted, since these countries (such as Bolivia) were allowed to proceed with negotiations for accession to the GATT.

8. U.S. document, "USSR and the General Agreement on Tariffs and Trade."

9. Statement by Soviet delegate at UN,ECE discussions, December 3, 1985.

10. Interviews 28, 29, 36, 37, 42, 78, and 127.

11. Interview 26.

12. Interview 127.

13. Interview 104; Margaret Chapman, ed., *Proceedings of an International Conference on "USSR Participation in the General Agreement on Tariffs and Trade (GATT)"* (Washington: American Committee on U.S.-Soviet Relations, 1989), p. 20; and William L. Richter, "Soviet 'Participation' in GATT: A Case For Accession," *New York University Journal of International Law and Politics*, vol. 20 (Winter 1988), pp. 497–98.

14. Interviews 1, 2, 17, 26, 36, 78, 95, 113, 120, and 124.

15. Interview 95.

16. GATT document L/6654. The application stated that "in order to examine the prerequisites of a future accession to the GATT, the Government of the USSR would like to get acquainted with the methods of work of various GATT bodies and to be able to keep GATT Contracting Parties regularly informed of the process of restructuring the economy of the Soviet Union." The Soviet offer to present regular reports on the process of economic restructuring was not conventional procedure in the GATT. Western governments had made it clear that they would expect increased information and periodic reports on developments in Soviet economic policy.

17. Interviews 132, 137, and 139. In these informal meetings Dunkel apparently made it clear that he hoped to see a positive decision taken on the matter during the council meeting scheduled for April or at the latest during the meeting scheduled for May. He also stressed that he did not consider it advisable for there to be any friction in the council meeting where the subject would be considered. Interview 139.

18. Interview 132.

19. Interview 141.

20. Interviews 141 and 142.

21. Interviews 141 and 143.

22. Interviews 131, 132, 136, and 137.

23. Interview 137.

24. Interviews 131, 132, 136, 137, and 139.

25. Interviews 131, 132, 137, and 141. The USTR had apparently attempted to obtain support for far more stringent clauses immediately after the Soviet application had been received. The USTR's proposal amounted to granting discriminatory observer status. It included restrictions on the meetings that the Soviet Union could attend, restrictions on the documents that the Soviet Union would have access to, and requirements for a review of the USSR itself after a trial two- or three-year period (rather than a review of the general question of observership). It seems that these proposals were quickly dropped when it became clear that the USTR was isolated in the U.S. government and in the international community.

Chapter 7

1. *Financial Times*, July 18, 1991, p. 4.

2. "Superpower Weapons Treaty First to Cut Strategic Bombs," *New York Times*, July 18, 1991, p. 1.

3. For a more detailed analysis of the extent to which and conditions under which GATT norms and rules influenced Western policymaking, see Leah Haus, "The East European Countries and GATT: The Role of Realism, Mercantilism and Regime Theory in Explaining East-West Trade Negotiations," *International Organization*, vol. 45 (Spring 1991), pp. 163–82.

4. Copies of the associate agreements reached with Yugoslavia and Poland can be found in Contracting Parties to the General Agreement on

Tariffs and Trade, *Basic Instruments and Selected Documents*, 8th Supplement (Geneva: GATT, 1960), pp. 11–14, 17–20.

5. For studies that consider the impact of membership in international economic institutions on the domestic politics of socialist countries, see Anne Dannenbaum, "The International Monetary Fund and Eastern Europe: The Politics of Economic Stabilization and Reform," Ph.D. dissertation, Yale University, 1989; and Harold K. Jacobson and Michel Oksenberg, *China's Participation in the IMF, the World Bank, and GATT: Toward a Global Economic Order* (University of Michigan Press, 1990).

6. Interview 53.

7. GATT document C/RM/S/10A, p. 34.

8. Richard E. Feinberg, "The Soviet Union and the Bretton Woods Institution: Risks and Rewards of Membership," Institute for East-West Security Studies, Public Policy Papers, 1989, p. 14.

9. Olivier Long, *Law and Its Limitations in the GATT Multilateral Trade System* (Dordrecht: Martinus-Nijhoff, 1985), p. 8.

10. This suggestion stems from a discussion with an interviewee.

11. Interviews 143 and 144.

12. Should other trade policy disputes arise with the Soviet Union's successor states in the context of the codes that are part of the GATT system, then a contracting party can easily take the matter to the codes' dispute settlement committees.

13. Interview 153.

14. The option of provisional accession was also used for Switzerland, although in this case, unlike others, tariff negotiations were no problem. The problem posed in the Swiss case involved quantitative restrictions applied against imports of agricultural products.

15. Gerard Curzon, *Multilateral Commercial Diplomacy* (London: Michael Joseph, 1965) p. 36; Kenneth W. Dam, *The GATT: Law and International Economic Organization* (University of Chicago Press, 1970), p. 347; and Interview 153.

16. Interview 153.

Index

Accession, protocol of. *See* Protocol of accession
Afghanistan, 1
Agreement on Technical Barriers to Trade. *See* Standards code
Agricultural policy, 56–57, 62
Albania, 2
Angola, 1
Article 35 (GATT): Soviet successor states' accession and, 114; U.S. use of, 38, 62, 67, 114
Australia, 39, 47; opposition to discriminatory QRs, 55, 57

Baker, James, 86
Belgium, 76
Benelux countries, 40; compromise on QRs and, 41
Bilateralism, 15, 24; article 24 and 18; EC-CMEA and, 63–64; EC–Eastern Europe and, 58–59, 63, 70, 99; EC-Hungarian agreement and, 65; EC-Rumanian agreement and, 59; EC-Soviet agreement and, 111; versus multilateralism, 34, 58–60; Poland's accession to GATT and, 31, 33; Soviet successor states' accession to GATT and, 107, 108; U.S. and Eastern countries, 66; U.S.-Soviet agreement and, 111
Bretton Woods Conference (*1944*), 90
British-Soviet agreement (*1930*), 23
Bulgaria, 2, 9; application for accession and, 80–88, 99; observer status and, 69; standards code and, 71–80; Uruguay Round and, 80–81
Bush administration, 67

Cambodia, 1
Canada, 39, 47, 75; bilateral agreement with U.S., 108; on bilateralism, 59; opposition to discriminatory QRs, 55, 57; Rumania's entrance fee and, 42, 61
China, 2; participation in Uruguay Round, 80, 81; relationship with GATT, 11
CMEA. *See* Council for Mutual Economic Assistance
Commercial considerations clause, 23, 89
Commission of European Communities: Hungarian accession and, 47; policy toward Bulgaria, 70, 74, 79
Committee on Technical Barriers to Trade, 79
Communism: Hungary and, 43
Containment policy, Western, 6; using economic tools for, 13
Coordinating Committee for Multilateral Export Controls (COCOM), 13
Council for Mutual Economic Assistance (CMEA), 1, 70; joint declaration with EC, 64, 82; policy toward EC, 63–64
Czechoslovakia, 2; MFN treatment by U.S., 67; relations with EC, 66

Declaration on Relations with Poland (*1959*), 27
de Gaulle, Charles, 14
Department of State, U.S.: position toward QRs, 33; Soviet observer status and, 95
Differentiation policy, 15, 25, 51, 70;

137